BEFORE YOU LOSE IT ALL
(Government and Freedom's Cultur`)

CONT`

CORRECTION: Line 6 from bottom of page 25—
   ". . . *none* of those visionary . . ."

BEFORE YOU LOSE IT ALL!

by David A. Norris

HEARTLAND PRESS
Box 305
Ames, Iowa 50010

Foreword

True American patriotism is a spiritual force. True liberty is only possible when dependence upon God is practiced. David Norris understands the virtual meaning of "one nation under God." He writes, therefore, not as a philosopher or theoretical historian, but as a Constitution-oriented, God-fearing American citizen with a practical insight into the principles that have made our nation great. *Before You Lose It All!* will provide clear political and spiritual direction in an area much in need of such clarity.

Mr. Norris has designed his book to assist the reader in analyzing the disastrous changes in American educational processes over the past sixty years. It documents the basic philosophy of the Declaration of Independence, the blessings which have been ours when true to that philosophy and the betrayal of that philosophy by modern leaders in politics and education. The author is both analytical and practical, informative and inspirational, concise and complete in his presentation. His suggestions for stimulating more Americans to strengthen true liberty by supporting private schools will be welcomed by observant and freedom-loving Americans everywhere.

5

Samuel F. Smith referred to "Our fathers' God" as the "Author of liberty." David Norris heartily agrees. The tone of America's culture with its standards of decency and self-discipline can again flourish according to the principles laid down by our founding fathers.

It is vitally important in the pursuit of our personal goals that we proceed with respect for these principles as they deserve to be respected. The truth is they have blessed us all more than any one of us deserve. The fact is the growing strength of those who would riddle our institutions and youth with degradation and immorality find their power in nothing more than our selfishness and confusion over the principles delineated in this book. Knowing this and desiring God's blessing should be the primary guide and basis for our daily walk. This is something too many learn too late in their grief. May God bless you as you become active and take a serious-minded approach to citizenship.

It is my privilege to commend this book to fellow Americans everywhere. From its reading, may a new standard be raised to the glory of God and the good of our beloved nation.

Paul Tassell, Ph.D., Pastor
Grandview Park Baptist Church
Des Moines, Iowa

ABOUT THE AUTHOR

David Norris traces his concern about trends in America to his military experiences during the Korean War and the rude awakening to what he did not know about the scarcity of liberty throughout history and what he did not know about socialism in North Korea and much of the world.

There developed an awareness of the mass of government intervention and manipulation of the production and resources of the people, irrespective of the necessity of human motivation to work.

Dave Norris is a grass-roots type of American, and this book comes from a groundswell of concern by the common people in our nation who believe something within that gave America unparalleled power and blessing has gone radically wrong.

A graduate of Iowa State University in agronomy and economics, he was the recipient of honorary scholastic membership to Alpha Zeta. As the foreman of the Story County Grand Jury in 1968, he was involved in an extensive study of problems in education reflected by campus lawlessness and disrespect for constitutional authority.

CHAPTER 1

Introduction

Seeing the American Bicentennial pass gives cause to reflect not only upon the basis of our greatness; but to ask what is the present status of these forces that determine the future?

A related question is, how are those who are calculating the demise of individual independence under just laws faring? Their counter-revolutionary attack takes on much of the same appearance as it did over two hundred years ago. But what is their progress and why? The English press emphasized in 1776 that the Declaration was badly prepared. One paper coined it "a wretched composition, very ill-written." Many Englishmen and political gossips believed the idea of God-given inalienable rights with individual responsibilities for government was absurd; instituted by a handful of rogues and opportunists who, of course, would come to no good. The new philosophy of government in the Declaration of Independence was treated by them as insignificant and ignored for the most part. Many years later when King George came face to face with Thomas Jefferson, he turned his back on Jefferson.

Our founders were far from perfect, but much wiser than the modern-day activists who concentrate on illuminating the founders' sins. Washington, Jefferson, Madison and the other leaders were acutely aware of the imperfections of men, in and out of power, and thus they established man over government and man under God whose commandments could be depended upon to sequester liberty.

Perhaps the greatest attack upon the integrity of our founders has been to attack the Declaration of Independence and deny that the Constitution was their implementation of the philosophy of the Declaration. The Revolution of 1776 in America based itself upon the just and moral reason for liberty and the just and moral reason for rejection of big government over man. Independence is two-fold: individual independence under God that resulted in great individual strength, and secondly, gave us national independence from control by Britain or any other country. America's principles that sequester liberty are based, of course, on the second and fourth sentences of the Declaration of Independence.

James Wilson, in the Pennsylvania ratifying convention, quoted from the first few lines of the Declaration of Independence and then said, "This is the broad basis on which our independence was placed; on the same certain and solid foundations this (United States Constitution) system is erected." Wilson's statement on the foundation or fundamental philosophy of American government is representative of the great amount of written testimony by our leaders who established it.

The discouragement among Americans, especially Biblical Christians over trends in society and the confusing inability to get corrections, can be cleared up by a re-examination of this unique heritage. The philosophy spelled out in the Declaration of Independence and implemented by our national Constitution has been sufficient; it is only a matter of returning to and reapplying those principles.

This destructive revolution has happened because Christians and others who believe in moral absolutes too often left socio-political involvement in education and government to others, not realizing their duty nor how extremely astute and adept some people are in controlling education and political trends left untended and unguarded. And second, as we see a breakdown of civilization in our nation we are frustrated and confused because our belated attendance to citizenship duties is ineffective in getting correction. This ineffectiveness is due to our failure to see the counter revolution and challenge it for what it really is, a censorship of the moral absolutes and honor due to the God of Creation, the very educational basis and core of America's greatness and power and liberty. The exclusion educationally from our consciousness of essential political and moral responsibility over the last sixty years is being energetically and deceptively imposed under the mantle of the ideal we love—liberty!! In order for us to succeed in the struggle for liberty, we need only to understand it anew and act firmly upon its principles!

As our nation enters its third century we see unprecedented illegitimacy, family breakdown, destruction of property, and insurrection against chains of authority.

Politicians fraternize with tyrants abroad who would destroy us and are destroying our allies one by one.

Politicians spend millions spreading their offices in our districts, acclaiming the good job they have done while catering to the irresponsibility of the unproductive. Solid, hard-working Americans find their liberty and self-sufficiency strangled by an ever growing tax burden.

Taxpayers are asked for more and more money for education, and it is spent as if our youth were a vast wasteland unworthy of absolutes and faith in God. Elected officials appoint judges who sidetrack laws that once severely punished people for violating our God-given right to life, liberty, and possessions. Business, industry, and the people have great problems with monopolizers that disturb or destroy the right to work and freedom of enterprise and marketing.

It is not hard to track these symptoms to the present breakdown in the tone of our culture and national posture to the counter-revolution.

America's hope for future greatness lies in the grass-roots self-education in the unique civilizing and liberating principles that were stressed educationally until the early 1900's. Our system of government still retains the procedures whereby the principles "Under God" can be reinstituted by the people. In understanding, there is power. Willful deception becomes powerless before serious patriots whose actions and opinions are stayed on the fundamentals of freedom's heritage.

"Patriotism is as much a virtue as justice, and is as necessary for the support of societies as natural affection is for the support of families. The *Amor Patriae* is both a moral and a religious duty. It comprehends not only the love of our neighbors but of millions of our fellow creatures, not only of the present but of future generations. This virtue we find constitutes a part of the first characters of history" (Dr. Benjamin Rush, An essay, 1773).

CHAPTER 2

Liberty Defined

Looking at liberty we find the simplest version in society is that men should have no restraints at all. But this, of course, leads to anarchy and in effect destroys liberty. Therefore, some internal and external restraints are necessary.

Looking first at the external or physical restraints, these would be unnecessary, if men were able to conduct themselves ethically at all times. Ethical behavior is conduct which respects the rights of others. If men were angels, no physical restraints or government would be necessary.

A synopsis of the meaning of the Declaration of Independence on this subject could read, freedom from the arm of the law or government dictation should come when men exercise self-restraint or self-responsibility out of respect for the Creator and the freedom of others within society. The best type of outer restraint is that which best reflects human nature and punishes those who use freedom maliciously. The punishment must be severe enough that the criminal will fear the punishment more than enjoy his selfish crimes.

We became one nation under God. This was a two-fold process—this Declaration coincided with the truth and gave God priority and secondly, faith in God gave substance to the

behavior of the governed. "From the day of the Declaration
... They (the American people) were bound by the laws of
God, which they all, and by the laws of the Gospel, which
they nearly all, acknowledged as the rules of their conduct"
(John Quincy Adams, Secretary of State, Oration celebrating
July 4, 1821).

The Declaration stated: "We hold these truths ... that men
... are endowed by their Creator with certain unalienable
rights: that among these are life, liberty, and the pursuit of
happiness: that to ensure these rights, governments are instituted among men."

This unique American ideal is, quite obviously, a political
concept with tremendous spiritual and economic overtones. It
is political in that rights to "life, liberty, and the pursuit of
happiness" are "unalienable," and the people have a right to
use force against others who would alienate these God-given
rights. The legitimate force of government is created by col-
lecting a small portion of each individual's right to use force
to protect his life, liberty and property.

It is spiritual in proclaiming the Creator as the endower of
men's rights and thus as sovereign. "I have lived, sir, a long
time, and the longer I live, the more convincing proofs I see
of this truth—*that God governs in the affairs of men.* And if
a sparrow cannot fall to the ground without His notice, it is
probable that an empire can rise without His aid? ... I also
believe that without His concurring aid we shall succeed in
this political building no better than the Builders of Babel ..."
(Benjamin Franklin, In Federal (Framing) Convention,
1787, making a motion for prayer). This basic principle im-
plicitly denies the state or a human elite as the endower of
men's rights, and thus the state or bureaucracy is not sovereign. ". . . the good people of the United States in their late
generous contest, contended for free government in the ful-
lest, clearest, and strongest sense. That they had no idea of
being brought under despotic rule under the notion of 'Strong
Government,' or in the form of *elective despotism:* Chains
being still chains, whether made of gold or iron. The corrupt-
ing nature of power, and its insatiable appetite for increase
... (makes amendments necessary to safeguard natural
rights)."* "The greatness of the powers given, and the multitude of places (offices) to be created produce a coalition ...

(dangerous to liberty and requiring) . . . such changes and securities as reason and experience prove to be necessary against the encroachments of power upon the indispensable rights of human nature."** (Richard Henry Lee, Letters to Samuel Adams* and George Mason** October, 1787).

The Declaration is an economic concept because it follows from men's inherent rights to sustain their lives, the sustenance of life being nothing more than the right to work and to have the fruits of this labor. The Declaration is spiritual, political and economic in that it did not promise happiness at the expense of others, only the environment of "liberty" for the "pursuit of happiness."

Liberty comes when each individual is educated to accept the responsibility to pursue happiness in his work and his relationship with God and man, not to be hindered by man or government. These principles have been the most contested ideals of government that exist because of what they do for those who believe, live and implement them; they liberate!! They keep the cause and effect relationship where it belongs—with man himself, and they liberate man from the delusion that he can have something for nothing without destroying freedom. Spiritual faith and freedom tend to rise and fall together. Like two mountain climbers securely tied to each other by a long rope, there is a "play" between them, and it is this "play" which permits one to help the other advance and which may keep the other from falling. Alexis de Tocqueville had a full appreciation of the point:

"I doubt that man can ever support at the same time complete religious independence (atheism or agnosticism) and entire political freedom. And I am inclined to think that if faith be wanting in him, he must be subject; and if he be free, he must believe."

If we lack this spiritual faith and do not understand the principles of 1776, our rights to life and liberty are placed on the altar of collective caprice, and they must suffer whatever fate the political apparatus dictates. The record clearly shows what this fate is. Russia is an example, yet practically every other nation, including our own, drifts in Russia's direction.

As adamant as our fathers were that there be separation of church and state, they were just as explicit in stressing in education and elsewhere the necessity of an atmosphere of respect and thanksgiving for the counsel of the nonsectarian God, Supreme Judge and Provider for individuals and nations. We have a restoration job on our hands. Freedom must experience a rebirth in America; that is, we must re-establish it from fundamental principles. Most of the bids aimed at a renewed freedom are far too low. Politics, education, more taxes, without God, all fall way short of the price of freedom. *Freedom is synonymous with genuine belief and walk with God.* Political collectivism and related types of man-made ideas are the antithesis of individual freedom and can be likened to a cancer.

Collectivists who would centrally control property, education, government, and business know precisely what they must do by any and all means—remove the God of liberty and moral absolutes from the classroom. Remove God from education under the mantle of ecclesiastical separation, or of liberty or of some other, such as academic freedom; and displace it with the daily emphasis of the secular religion of socialism, "social this and social that." They say that education assures liberty, but education does not assure liberty. Education is the tool by which the doctines of liberty are known or subverted teachings become the means of frustrating liberty.[1] When a new generation is persuaded that socialism exists by its own right even with oppressive taxation and outrageous legislation, leaders can rule. They rule by the ignorance in which the people are held, ignorance of the sovereignty of

[1] William Safire, "Disquiet, Please," *New York Times*, August 11, 1975. (Sample of distortion and censorship)

"At a cost to taxpayers of $220,189.00 some eight million copies of a reading list are being distributed which testify to the intellectual and political bias of a group of librarians who evidently seek to rig the discussion of American issues by tilting the 'approved' materials leftward.

". . . there is something very wrong about a pretense of debate: framing a 'dialogue' with materials that preordain the winners, supported mainly by dollars from the predetermined losers.

". . . 'balance' . . . the list, in its totality, reveals the bias of the people who control the purchase and display of a large portion of the books published in this country.

"If the librarians can get away with suppression of untrendy ideas, then the 'American Issues Forum' will be seen by the people who hold the library cards as a national brainwashing."

God and ignorance of lesser responsibilities and simple duties of individual conduct by which they can be free. To say that any people are not fit for freedom is to make subjection their lot and to choose for them the load of heavy oppression. If such a case could be proven, it would equally prove that those who govern are not fit to govern, for they are of the same species—man.

The second group of restraints are the inner restraints which men impose on themselves: random impulses, urges, whims, and compulsions are all sorted, graded, policed or checked by man himself. To whatever extent actions are restrained, to that extent the person's total freedom is lost. If an uninhibited expression means destroying property or educational mischief—stimulating the sexual drive of youngsters in the classroom, or disclosing national security secrets in the press, that would be classified as "freedom" to those who would want no restraints. If asked to explain his actions the person might say, "Well, it seemed like a good idea." He might take a stand on the deism of English philosophy or some other philosophy to counter or displace Judeo-Christian claims to know right from wrong through the revelation of God. He might proclaim skepticism as a philosophical basis for emancipating humanity from responsibility and obligations to God and country. True liberty has some very definite limits.

The American heritage of political and economic freedom is foreign to the minds of those who now advocate our throwing off those liberty-preserving restraints they ridicule as "old restraints" or needless inhibitions. This counter-revolutionary movement would subvert freedom's principles of right and wrong, rewarding the irresponsible and penalizing the good; destroying our institutions and their ability to protect our life and liberty for the pursuit of happiness. While on one hand these new revolutionaries advocate emancipation of the press, emancipation of the mind and emancipation of education from any absolutes, they promote more and more government controls and restraints over the resources and business pursuits of the people.

The Declaration of Independence is a fundamental and uniquely American recognition of Divine Origin as the basis for society and government. When understood, this neutralizes the power of secular humanist philosophies and the so-called divine right of socialists, kings, etc.[2] ". . . I fully agree in Opinion with a very celebrated Author that 'Freedom or Slavery will prevail in a (City or) Country according to the Disposition and Manners of the People render them fit for the one or the other,' and I have long been convinced that our Enemies have made it an Object to eradicate from the Minds of the People in general a Sense of true Religion and Virtue, in hopes thereby the more easily to carry their Point of enslaving them. Indeed my Friend, this is a Subject so important in my Mind, that I know not how to leave it. Revelation assures us that 'Righteousness exalteth a Nation'—Communities are dealt with in this World by the wise and just Ruler of the Universe. He rewards or punishes them according to their general Character. The diminution of publick Virtue is usually attended with that of publick Happiness, and the publick Liberty will not long survive the total Extinction of Morals" ("convincd" in the original, Samuel Adams, Letter to John Scollay, 1776).

The Spirit of 1776, or the Creator concept, elevates the masses of common men above and beyond the reach of those highminded who want to deceive their minds and manipulate their lives. Men's rights were tied to God-given principles rather than humanistic rationalization. The family was strengthened —not undermined, Our God-given rights are limited—liberty is unavoidably tied to responsibility, responsibility to respect the Creator and his commandments that protect the equal rights of others. Divine Origin is fundamental. Our American constitutional system is structured so those who wished to be happy and have material abundance by taking it from others

2 Secular used here refers to that belonging to things materialistic, and worldly, standing in opposition to things based upon the nonsectarian God, Judge of nations and Creator of man. It could be defined as the endeavor of the creature to act as though he created himself and as though no divine benefactor and law giver existed. Whatever the cause, be it selfishness, rebellion, be it lack of knowledge of the Spirit of 1776, victims of educational mischief, censorship, etc., the individuals use humanistic theories, such as situation ethics and evolution, endeavoring to legitimatize controlling their own little world, devoid of God. Although the secular humanist rejects the justice, the morality, the great love, human goodness and progress that comes with trust in God, he uses these words liberally in counterfeit to wrangle positions for his objectives.

and avoiding personal responsibility suffered severe consequences. This was not to deny a subsistence program for those who were really physically incapable or mentally incompetent. The Judeo-Christian principle emphasizes the responsibility of setting aside a tenth of the economic produce for these people.

Christian citizens' responsibilities should include participation in the local church, in political activities, and in an education program. Even though they are not directly connected, work in one complements the other, and the negligence by Christians in the one ultimately will lead to the destruction of the other as far as freedom and national blessing goes. A balance is important; if all Christian adults participated in precinct meetings, inquiring of candidates' stands on crucial issues and voting, comparatively little time would be necessary. If God extends a specific calling to politics, even this need not detract more than in other occupations from one's personal witness and work through the local church. Serving God through the church as well as minimal civic duties needs to be a continuing service in order to get and keep an atmosphere conducive to honoring God. People do not plan to lose their freedom; they lose their freedom because they fail in planning to give these duties sufficient status importance.

CHAPTER 3

Historical Parallels

The secular revolution we are now experiencing has many parallels in history—one being the French Revolution and another the German of this century. Edmund Burke, the English statesman who resisted King George III and defended the American Colonies, turned against the French Revolution from its very beginning. As early as 1773, after visiting France, he warned the English Parliament that those *speculative rationalist philosophers* would "degrade us into brutes." Thus, before the outbreak of either revolution, and long before the fall of the Bastille in 1789, Burke had decided in favor of America and against France. The Germanies of the early 1900's and again in the 1930's and 1940's and the French Revolution that came into focus in the 1780's proclaimed their "Divine Mission," their "Super Race," their "Republic of Virtue." Their universities, their music, their arts, their science and philosophy excelled. Illiteracy was at an irreducible minimum among the German people. The French Jacobians tried to fix over everything: fashions, literature, drama, even the calendar—renaming the months and acclaiming a new reckoning rather than the new birth through Christ.

Likewise, here in America over the last sixty years our wisdom and unique principles that elevate man to self-responsibility and control over his own destiny must be fixed over; so, we see new phonics, new math, new economics, new history, as well as new morality, new principles of government and secular humanist god with no moral absolutes. This has given us poor spellers, less math comprehension, economies of insolvency, loss of history's significance, moral deterioration, massive collectivist government. Educational abandonment of the absolutes of morality and trust in God after the great blessings of God on America are testimony to the frailty of human leadership. Should it continue, it would represent one of the greatest travesties upon a heritage and one of the greatest blunders of all time. If there is no alternative to regaining our principles, we ought to abandon public education and place our children in private schools where love of God, morality and country are taught! When the state education does not support the philosophy of the Constitution and will not, it is time to exercise a new declaration of independence and turn to private education no matter what the cost.

The French and German experiences in scuttling the wisdoms of the ages are illustrative of counter-revolution in America today. The German and French, advocates of a heaven on earth which contributed to the ruin of great peoples, were among the most titanic tragedies of the ages. Few would deny, as Burke once warned of the French philosophers, that the speculative rationalist philosophers here in America are making "brutes" of us. As then, the counter-revolutionaries of today attack the people with a diatribe acclaiming the footdraggers as guilty for an imperfect society. The intellectual reformers in these French and German epochs found that their ordinary, unimaginative, radical commoners simply could not be made over into proper citizens of their projected utopia. When they got complete political control, they did the only thing left to them. Like the communist visionaries of today, they proceeded to exterminate the misfits. The aims of our founding fathers were quite prosaic and mundane by contrast. To the founding fathers of this Republic heaven was in the next life; the task of government was earthly and limited and so they wisely wanted it kept.

Edmund Burke recognized the danger of education devoted entirely to the discovery of knowledge, without regard for the will and intention of the Creator of man; that the counter-revolution's definition of liberty—emancipation from the centuries' proven principles of right and wrong—has failed, is obvious. History's parallels give ample demonstration of the ruin that lurks in the wake of mere emancipated minds. Even ethical teachings and morality, though helpful, will not suffice. Moral philosophy may be similar to other knowledge but it is not the force that controls the acts and liberates men from selfishness. It takes a positive belief in the God who made us and loves us more than we love ourselves. "Experience is a severe perceptor, but it teaches useful truths, and however harsh, is always honest. Be calm and dispassionate, and listen to what it tells us" (Chief Justice of New York, John Jay, Address to People of New York State, 1788). History must record our returning to God if liberty is to survive.

The God of Creation is very patient. In His divine perfection He most graciously extended to His created beings an option of returning this love and fellowship. Man chose to reject God, and sin was born. God did not want it this way, but it was by man's choice. What is commonly called the "good news" is that in spite of our rejection of God, "For God so loved the world that he gave his only begotten son (Jesus who knew no sin and died on the cross for our sins) that whosoever believeth in him (invites Christ into his life as Lord and Savior) should not perish, but have everlasting life (saved from the penalty of sinful deeds into fellowship and abundant blessing with God here and in heaven)." (John 3:16)

Who is the most outstanding personality of all time? Jesus of Nazareth. History has recorded no other who has changed all reference to time as Christ has—B.C., meaning before Christ and A.D. *(anno Domini)*, meaning "in the year of our Lord."

The true message of Christ has always produced changed lives. Men see justice as a friend and not as inhumane; self-discipline becomes a sought after goal consistent with truth. These changed lives have produced lasting changes in nations.

One writer described His influence in this way: "Nineteen wide centuries have come and gone and today He is the centerpiece of the human race and the leader of the column of progress. I am far within the mark when I say that all the armies that ever marched and all the navies that ever were built, and all of the parliaments that ever have sat, and all the kings that ever reigned put together have not affected the life of man upon this earth as powerfully as has that one solitary life, Jesus of Nazareth!"

Christ never quoted philosophers. It is men who know there is truth in Christ that quote Him. The commands of God and opportunity to worship Him are not for God's benefit, they are to man's benefit. God does not need our worship, men need it, and in love God gave us some very helpful commands. "God that made the world and all things therein, seeing that he is Lord of heaven and earth, dwelleth not in temples made with hands; Neither is worshipped with men's hands, as though he needed any thing, seeing he giveth to all life, and breath, and all things; And hath made of one blood all nations of men for to dwell on all the face of the earth, and hath determined the times before appointed, and the bounds of their habitation; That they should seek the Lord, if haply they might feel after him, and find him, though he be not far from every one of us: For in him we live, and move, and have our being; as certain also of your own poets have said, For we are also his offspring. Forasmuch then as we are the offspring of God, we ought not to think that the Godhead is like unto gold, or silver, or stone, graven by art and man's device. And the times of this ignorance God winked at; but now commandeth all men every where to repent: Because he hath appointed a day, in the which he will judge the world in righteousness by *that* man whom he hath ordained; *whereof* he hath given assurance unto all *men*, in that he hath raised him from the dead." (Acts 17:24–31)

CHAPTER 4

Debt Will Destroy

A priority of humanity throughout history has been life, liberty, and possessions. The major stumbling block to this goal is having the capacity to resist the subterfuge of social planners who make glittering promises in exchange for the control of God-given rights and the fruits of man's labor.

"Kings or parliaments could not give the rights essential to happiness . . . We claim them from a higher source—from the King of kings, and Lord of all the earth. They are not annexed to us by parchments and seals. They are created in us by the decrees of Providence . . . It would be an insult on the divine Majesty to say, that he has given or allowed any man or body of men a right to make me miserable. If no man or body of men has such a right, I have a right to be happy. If there can be no happiness without freedom, I have a right to be free. If I cannot enjoy freedom without security of property, I have a right to be thus secured" (John Dickinson, Reply to a Committee in Barbadoes, 1766).

The liberty and possessions of the working citizens are destroyed through usurious taxation-inflation and by promoting irresponsibility in able-bodied citizens with handouts that make work seem unnecessary and justice a mockery.

24

The pillars for liberty are embedded in the belief in the Biblical God who promotes not only morality, but adherence to the work ethic. "For even when we were with you, this we commanded you, that if any would not work, neither should he eat" (2 Thess. 3:10). The economics of liberty require honest accommodation to these basic truths, well summarized by the American Economic Foundation in the following four paragraphs:

Nothing in our material world can come from nowhere or go nowhere, nor can it be free: everything in our economic life has a source, a destination and a cost that must be paid.

Government is never a source of goods. Everything produced is produced by the people, and everything that government gives to the people, it must first take from the people.

The only valuable money that government has to spend is that money taxed or borrowed out of the people's earnings. When government decides to spend more than it has thus received, that extra unearned money is created out of thin air, through the banks, and, when spent, takes on value only by reducing the value of all money and savings.

The productivity of the tools—that is, the efficiency of the human energy applied in connection with their use—has always been highest in a competitive society in which the economic decisions are made by millions of progress-seeking individuals, rather than in a state-planned society in which those decisions are made by a handful of all-powerful people, regardless of how well-meaning, unselfish, sincere and intelligent those people may be.

The economics of liberty are very practical. They have one of those visionary and unrealistic goal levels used by communists and other secular strategists to bait the victims of censorship into working for the exchange of liberty and yielding up the fruit of their labor.

Government power to take from the working citizens a tax to be given to non-workers for daily living must be strictly limited. Those who honestly, and without fabrication, have a need because they are physically or mentally incapable and have no honorable alternative, should be the recipients of a modest welfare program. Redistribution of wealth, however, by government beyond the limit of absolute needs is legalized pilferage, a form of injustice, social corruption and political subversion over people.

Work is a form of pain for each individual, the price the Creator intends for material progress and the honorable way in society to gain material possessions. Because of the human genius for conniving and deception to avoid work, it is not even possible for bureaucrats to know who honestly is and is not in legitimate need. Their well-intentioned subordinates serving on welfare staffs are constantly frustrated in their efforts to get proper control.

Welfare decisions on the legitimacy of need should be returned to the local citizens who pay the bills and will greatly reduce abuses. Then beach bums, slackers, roving husband voters, as well as collectivist politicians, will again have the incentive to work and to be a part of the solution rather than the problem. Such decisions could be handled locally by citizen committees selected at random, removed from politics; a simplification of the system of jury selection we use to judicate criminal allegations.

Unemployment assistance properly handled has an important role in the responsible, free society. With the tremendous benefits of free enterprise comes the necessity of phasing out enterprises that are no longer profitable, and needed by the consumer. This causes shifts in employment, the need for workers to establish themselves in different jobs or move to a different location.

The enormous problems in the present system could be minimized if unemployment insurance were removed from short-term political control to alleviate vote-buying, if restructured, so it is absolutely without any political gimmickry, paying its own way and, thirdly, private enterprise given the freedom to compete, providing the same benefits and serving to decentralize power.

Unemployment benefits should be on a matching funds, or some similar, basis. Too often the unemployed will not take a job because the jobs available are in another skill and the wages less than the unemployment benefit. The matching fund approach would require that they work somewhere to receive any benefit at all, and their unemployment benefits could match dollar for dollar what they earn on a temporary job up to a modest limit. This, along with moving allowance when necessary, would reduce the present cost significantly and get people into productivity. One of the most unpublicized statistics in America today is the number of jobs seeking workers. Millions of these jobs would be filled, and some workers would find the new work to their liking and challenge to a new career.

". . . a Public Debt is a Public curse, and in a Rep Govt a greater than any other" (James Madison, Letter to Henry Lee, 1790) (Note: "Rep Govt" means that of a Republic). Speaking of King James III in the Declaration of Independence, Jefferson wrote, "He has erected a multitude of New Offices, and sent hither swarms of Officers to harass our people, and eat out their substance" (Declaration of Independence).

For most of the two hundred years of our existence as a nation, the policy of the United States government has been to use public credit only in times of war, or in a dire national emergency. From George Washington down to Franklin Roosevelt the attitude of our Presidents was to keep the nation solvent. Debt was taken seriously. This attitude prevailed in settling the bills for the American Revolution and it prevailed in all others wars until World War II.

The United States has a growth rate, expressed in our Gross National Product the last two years, which was smaller than any other industrialized nation in the world. This nation is producing less than 70% of capacity and the outlook for investment to increase that capacity is bleak as the incentive for people to work and save is gradually destroyed through collectivism. While the federal government was on an all-time high of deficit spending, many state and local governments are also moving toward bankruptcy.

At the close of business fiscal 1976 the national debt stood at a staggering 646.4 billion. In what is becoming a trend, your government spent 66.5 billion dollars beyond its income during fiscal 1976.

Inflation from excess spending, the most vicious tax of all, leaches away the purchasing power and the saving of the old and young alike. We pay an even greater price in loss of character as programs get legislated that tempt citizens to become spongers.

Long before the 1960's when violence began to issue from our campuses, tyrants of the mind were gaining a following and the victims of censorship clamoring for utopian goals in ecology, health, safety, welfare, etc., with the subsequent debasing effect. Very sincere and well-intentioned citizens are falling in line as collectivist master-minds succeed in the control of humanities education. Ignorant, they see these unrealistic goal levels in terms of a divine right of Kings to take away the independence of the common men and women. The American system, with government limited in taxing and regulating powers, gives the common people status to enjoy life and progress, learning from running their own affairs. Wherever the controls, the money, and ownership are vested, that is where the power is. American principles, when implemented, are unique at this point; the common people have the power, and the would-be government elite are kept down. Governments historically have been just the opposite. Instead of our rights coming from God, this divine prerogative is taken by government collectivists who would force us to submit to their surveillance and come to them to get authority for the exercise of a right to live, to own property, and to use it.

Private ownership of property (capital formation), for instance, is now receiving very damaging blows from pressure point politics at local, state and regional levels.[1] The benefits of capital formation by and for our citizens could be compared to tenure granted to professors by some universities. They both give freedom, financial security and protection from the outside. The consequence of taxing, spending and

[1] USA Special Report on Columbia University Riots by Alice Widener, 1968. Article elaborates upon the planning of "pressure point politics" of a noisy minority to get regulation and control of business "by states and cities." Purpose—to destroy capital formation at its "roots."

Ames Daily Tribune, March 18, 1977, ". . . industry crippled . . ." Example: ". . . in 1970 nearly 50 per cent of the American population could afford a medium priced house. In 1976, that figure had dropped to 25 per cent."

regulating away this right of the common people is obvious, as is the impact of allowing independence for only a few so-called elite.

Some politicians try to explain away the trends of the last twenty-five years by saying, "Aren't you living better than any previous generation of Americans, why worry?" This explanation is born either of ignorance or deceit. Others deny, with halos over their heads, responsibility for spending excesses that jeopardize freedom. Their promises are always redeemed by forcing sacrifices from the working men and women, but few of these politicians have the courage to suggest the wage earner take a 5% or 10% reduction in pay. Freedom calls for Congressmen who understand, want a balanced budget, and will bargain on no other basis.

Just as important, those of us who have accepted government subsidies need to realize the harm that is being done to our future well-being and the very present danger to freedom caused by government debt.

Living better, while creating bigger debts, is little solace to nations that collapse, as did New York City, but with no one to bail them out. If it were your next-door neighbor spending 20% above his income year by year, you know well what would ultimately happen. That is just what our whole nation is doing. We are joyously and rapidly moving toward ruin.

James Madison was concerned about government over people when he said, "Although all men are born free, and all nations might be so, yet too true it is, that slavery has been the general lot of the human race. Ignorant—they have been cheated; asleep—they have been surprised; divided—the yoke has been forced upon them. But what is the lesson? That because the people may betray themselves, they ought to give themselves up, blindfold, to those who have an interest in betraying them? Rather conclude that the people ought to be enlightened, to be awakened, to be united, that after establishing a government they should watch over it, as well as obey it" (Essay: "Who Are the Best Keepers of the People's Liberties?" 1772).

Just as any specific ideology, communism, for instance, is dependent upon educational indoctrination to keep the masses yoked to the central government; the strength of America's system of citizen independence and limited government is absolutely dependent upon education faithfully teaching the economics of liberty where individuals, as well as governments, live within their means.

CHAPTER 5

Education Versus Tyrants of the Mind

Education is a beautiful word. It comes from the Latin *educaare*, which means to rise up, to take from the lowest degrees to the highest spheres of knowledge. America's founding fathers were unwavering advocates of unique and educationally demonstrable principles for man and government. Without them, liberty would not have been possible. To the founders, education was not a vast wasteland, as it is, but rather the life or death of liberty. They helped institute education free of the haze and cloudy confusion usable by politicizers and tyrants of the mind. Jefferson stated, "I have sworn upon the altar of God, eternal hostility against every form of tyranny over the mind of man."

God implanted in the bosom of humanity the thirst and the aspiration for new and great destinies. Education consistent with the Creator, mentioned in the Declaration of Independence, enables people to assimilate the eternal principles that foster responsible individual behavior and gives the will and the discernment to see through and reject shallow promises. The existence of liberty is, by its very definition, dependent on an educational environment that encourages the belief in the minds of the youth in the God of creation and justice and

31

His moral law. Education that does not consistently undergird our nation's Constitution with belief in God and our founding principles, upon which religious conviction and patriotism in the private sector may consistently develop, is nihilistically defective.

Today when only approximately 19% of the world's population live in freedom by our standards, one-fourth of which is America itself, it is important to visualize how little liberty has ever existed throughout history. It should never be forgotten also that the fundamental American principles of government were the results of generations of painful experience in self-government in America prior to 1776 and were not mere theories drawn from books, but practical principles. This is true of the principles of the Declaration of Independence as well as our constitutional system.

". . . as yet, philosophical generalization upon abstract questions of the highest class is not the characteristic of the American mind" (John Adams, "Thoughts on Government" 1778). This quality has, of course, made it very hard for revolutionaries to subvert Americans away from their principles and only in the past sixty years have they met with much success.

A distinct concern of America's leaders who established our nation upon specific principles was expressed by George Washington in his Farewell Address, ". . . batteries of internal and external enemies will be most constantly and actively directed, . . . much pains will be taken, many artifacts employed to weaken your minds . . ."

Historically, politicized groups—military, clergy and others—controlling the flow of information negating or censoring established truth have been the outstanding method used to enslave the masses. Presently, tyranny of the mind is being imposed upon us in the name of, and in the disguise of, that status we cherish most—LIBERTY!!!!!!!!!

Without the benefit of specific principles and absolutes of morality in education, it is common to have two people taking opposing positions publicly on such issues as abortion, capital punishment, a balanced budget, or sexual fidelity, and have them both claiming scientific proof in support of their views.

Fostering a knowledge spectrum devoid of the specific principles of government and absolutes in morality is a tyranny that denies the people their freedom because it leaves them unable to discern and act on principles that make it possible for millions of people to share in a complex society and still have liberty.

Belief in God was basic to education for the one hundred thirty years or so both before and after the Declaration of Independence of 1776. The Declaration, in spelling out the American philosophy of government, referred to the Creator four times. Teachers and textbooks supported "One Nation Under God" without becoming sectarian.

Even the liberal historian Henry Steele Commager gives education prior to 1900 some credits. We would differ with his use of the world allusion and his conclusion about luckless predecessors, but these comments extracted from the foreword to *McGuffey's Sixth Reader* tell about the educational emphasis that existed for most of our nation's history.

"One thing the McGuffey Readers shared with schoolbooks everywhere, and indeed with most literature and art of their day—the notion that education itself was primarily moral, and only secondarily intellectual. . . . The world of the McGuffeys was a world where no one questioned the truths of the Bible, or their relevance to everyday conduct, where the notion that the separation of church and state required the exclusion of religion from the schoolroom or from schoolbooks seemed preposterous. The Readers, therefore, are filled with stories from the Bible, and tributes to its truth and beauty. . . . William McGuffey showed no awareness in his Readers, or in his college and university teaching, of those progressive educational ideas that had their origins in Germany, penetrated into France and England, and spread to New England, . . ."[1]

In the prospectus of *The Youth's Companion* dated 1827, " 'this is the day of peculiar care for Youth. Let their minds be formed, their hearts prepared, and their characters moulded for the scenes and duties of a brighter day.' And when Franklin Edmunds launched a little series of books for boys he assured anxious parents that 'all stories of an exaggerated

[1] From the foreword to McGUFFEY'S SIXTH READER by Henry Steele Commager. Copyright © 1964 by The New American Library of World Literature, Inc. By arrangement with the New American Library, Inc., New York, N. Y. pp. vii, viii, vii.

style and false sentiment will be avoided and nothing presented but what will be calculated to inculcate some moral lessons.' . . . God was omnipresent."[2] "In the substantial attention the McGuffeys gave to American literature, in the celebration—or at least the affectionate recollection—of Washington and Franklin, Patrick Henry, and Daniel Webster, they contributed no doubt to fostering a sense of patriotism in the young. But there was no deliberate attempt to do this."[3]

"It is here that the Readers made, perhaps, their greatest contributions, and it is here that they have something to teach us. For one of the things that has gone out of much of current study of literature and history on the elementary level is this common body of allusion and of reference. That our children, today, are better taught than were their luckless predecessors is generally conceded, though we are sometimes puzzled that we have not produced a generation of statesmen as distinguished as the Founding Fathers—products of rural academies and embryo colleges . . .[4] The McGuffey Readers, then, are far more than a historical curiosity. They played an important role in American education, and in American culture, and helped shape that elusive thing we call the American character. If they did not themselves provide the stuff of culture and morality, they were one of the chief instruments for weaving this stuff into the fabric of American life. Their contribution was, on the whole, a beneficent one.[5] They gave to the American child of the nineteenth century what he so conspicuously lacks today—a common body of allusions, a sense of common experience and of common possession."[6]

Public education was consistent with (1) the separation of sectarian church hierarchical powers from the powers of state: (2) the need of an educational base for general belief in God in support of America's unique Constitution, man under God and over government: (3) the need of state schools being separated from the *apostate tyrants of the mind* who would use state powers to politicize education in fulfillment

---

2 *McGuffey's Sixth Reader*, p. ix.
3 *McGuffey's Sixth Reader*, p. xiii.
4 *McGuffey's Sixth Reader*, p. xiv-xv.
5 *McGuffey's Sixth Reader*, p. xvi.
6 Commager's foreword to *McGuffey's Sixth Reader*. (New York: The American Library, 1962), p. xiv.

of their goals to enslave by undermining belief in God and moral absolutes.

Education under control of one religious group always leads to the suppression of the others, so separation of church and state has proven essential to liberty. It is important that we see and understand that communism and related sects who get the upper hand in education are much more devastating upon freedom than the historic church and state marriage we oppose. Education satisfactory to atheistic and related sects of secular humanism leads new generations to conclude that God is relatively unimportant to life's principles and becomes the rival of belief in the God of creation and Judge of nations as well as being the enemy of political and economical independence. Cultural and moral education, whatever it is, is going on day by day as a continual process in every classroom and in every activity. "Education simply is not value free."[7] This is an inescapable truth. Education that is soft or abandons the principles of liberty, morality, and responsibility becomes a tool for propaganda, moral pollution and political subversion; and if continued will make liberty impossible.

Teachers who stress belief in the Creator and the specific and unique American principles are presented as a tyranny to academic freedom and enlightened liberty. Justice becomes inhumane, unsuited for education doctrine and is replaced with an obscurity for collectivist manipulation. Academic centers become a centrifuge for socialist propaganda. Sincere and sound objections to communism by anyone are labeled McCarthyism with connotations that elicit stay-away-from-that feelings. Strictness in discipline, manners, and grammar become passé. Students who refuse to get involved in the new morality and stand firm for strong, loyal marriages are squares and needlessly short-circuiting their rights. National pride in America gets labeled as selfish isolationism and dangerous to the world union. The ability to gouge the government for a free handout shows that one is smart. Truly responsible school boards are labeled as weak in academic excellence and as bigots too small in their thinking. Textbooks that are free of sectarian doctrine and coercion but stress reli-

[7] David Purpel and Kevin Ryan, "Moral Education—Where Sages Fear to Tread," *Phi Delta Kappan*, June 1975—Later in *Education Digest*, November 1975.

ance upon God in life are labeled falsely as a violation of separation of church and state. The term "reason," instead of being the useable definitive term, becomes a word for the "age of the great philosophers" that left God out. Creation of man by God is discounted or discredited while the theory that man accidentally came through evolution is shown great respect.

ABSENCE OF AMERICAN PRINCIPLES DESTROYING THE HOME

Upon one pillar, the family unit, more than any other, stands each individual's development, strength and independence for prosperity. A key factor affecting the survival of a strong family is the standard for sexual behavior. Quoting the historians Will and Ariel Durant in *The Lessons of History*, ". . . . no one man, however brilliant or well-informed, can come in one lifetime to such fullness of understanding as to safely judge and dismiss the customs or institutions of his society, for these are the wisdom of generations after centuries of experiment in the laboratory of history. A youth boiling with hormones will wonder why he should not give full freedom to his sexual desires. If he is unchecked by custom, morals or laws, he may ruin his life before he matures sufficiently to understand that sex is a river of fire that must be banked and cooled by a hundred restraints if it is not to consume in chaos both the individual and the group."[8]

If one wanted to destroy human dignity and the personal

[8] Will and Ariel Durant, *The Lessons of History* condensed in *Reader's Digest*, December 1968, p. 268. (New York: Simon and Schuster, 1968).

Reader's Digest Introduction to the Lessons of History—"This book is the culmination of one of the great scholarly achievements of our time, a ten-volume series. The Story of Civilization, hailed by the eminent historian Allan Nevins as 'one of the outstanding works of American historiography.' Over the 40 years since the Durants began their researches, more than three million copies of the volumes in the series have been sold.

"The Lessons of History is the summary of this monumental enterprise, the distillation of what the experience of 20 civilizations over a period of 4,000 years can tell us about man's long journey through war, conquest, creation and self-exploration."

freedom and force the people to willingly accept a dictatorship, the family would be a logical place to attack. Having strong family ties and high sexual ethics in the first place, it would be wise to bypass the parents and strike at the most vulnerable point—the captive audience of inexperienced youth.

With the decision to destroy the sexual ethic through curriculum changes in the public schools and universities, the next action must secure the support of the youth and dissuade the teachers and the parents from opposition. Three simple excuses to involve curriculum could be—there is some venereal disease, some illegitimacy, and sexual maladjustment in some marriages. Then the enemies of responsible freedom would attack by unleashing the river of fire from the restraints of society by (1) destroying the natural modesty and the protective cloak of personal dignity and sacredness in which sex is held by boys and girls, (2) overpowering the ability to contain themselves sexually until they establish a sound relationship of marriage, (3) discrediting God and belief in His teachings of right and wrong. The attack would be or is multilateral through textbooks in physical education, health, science, arts, literature, and social studies. The focal point for the attack would be sex education. Youth would be told explicitly of the sensual and physical gifts which God meant for marriage and which in a strong society are introduced at the time of marriage. Luring stories and wicked possibilities that could not possibly reach the mind of youth without some adult implanting them would be taught under the banner of literature and art. "They ought to know." The communication of evil is not new, but in this way the enemies of freedom would have the sanction of the educators to use the classroom. In other words, they would reverse the use to which education was put until recently; that of using literature and art to support moral absolutes and one nation under God.

If one wanted to destroy the sexual ethics of a nation, he would want to establish substitutes for the powerful forces of restraint represented by blunt and continual warnings of the terrible mental, physical, and social repercussions of venereal disease, pregnancy out of wedlock, and judgment of God. These substitutes would include great emphasis on the benefits of medical treatment, contraceptives and relief services for unwed mothers. The running battle would need two or three generations to sufficiently pollute and get popular support for the removal of laws and traditions. They would want an alliance with any academic group or union that would help remove the control of the curriculum from the adult taxpayers. School codes of conduct that set good standards of propriety for students and use of school dorms must be eliminated. Pimp codes that "liberate" and allow illicit sexual activity among students in publicly owned school dormitories must be enforced by school administrators. People would be screened who pursue advanced degrees in curriculum management and teacher training to be sure that those who reject nihilistic ideas in favor of traditional cultural emphasis do not get higher degrees.

To destroy the family through education, the classroom must be free from parental power to stop teaching that which encourages immorality and political subversion. Governmental changes must be made so the selection and tenure of teachers and their superintendents will be removed from the ballot box and sensitive local control. The students and public must be encouraged to worship education, holding it up as being above political recourse and beyond the realm of criticism. The counter-revolutionaries could also use economy as an excuse. When the public sees the rising cost of education, the increase in moral decay and divorce rate, they would be prepared with new reasons for emancipating the minds of the youth from moral responsibility. They would also want to deter thought patterns leading to the popularization of small locally controlled schools giving parents and taxpayers strong control. The above techniques would ultimately accomplish the destruction of liberty, and to the extent that they are going on today we are seeing the decay of our civilization.

Americans want liberty and not dictatorship or minds emancipated for liberty without moral responsibility.

ACADEMIC RESPONSIBILITY—REFRESHING

The basically distinct difference in the American principles of government for education are evident in the writings of

Washington, Madison, Jefferson, John Adams, Patrick Henry and many others.

A conclusive example among others as to the acceptance by our leaders of a certain set of principles as being fundamentally American, is found in the resolution offered and implemented by the University of Virginia in March of 1825. This resolution that was adopted by the University board was proposed by James Madison, often called "The father of the Constitution" because of his influence in forming the Federal Constitution in 1787, and Thomas Jefferson. These two were members of the Board of Visitors, and Jefferson was the Rector or head of the University of Virginia at the time.

The resolution stated that all students shall be inculcated (indoctrinated) with the basic American principles of government and that "none should be inculcated (indoctrinated) which are incompatible with those on which the Constitution of this State, and of the United States were genuinely based, in the common opinion." The faculty had a standard of *responsibility* and *was required to teach positively and affirmatively these unique American principles*; then and only then, they were to teach the conflicting principles as such being judged by the soundness of the American principles that served as a basis. This is an indispensable duty aspect of Academic Freedom-Responsibility, which is closely related to Individual Liberty-Responsibility in general. Otherwise, the students are deprived of the substance of their right to freedom of choice; the right to know the whys and wherefores of freedom, including its foundation in the Judeo-Christian philosophy.

The other leaders who helped establish our nation in liberty undoubtedly agreed with these two outstanding contributors, Jefferson and Madison, on this point. In order for the benefits of liberty to survive, the unique American principles must be stressed in a positive way to the uninformed youth of new generations. In this way, new generations would have a clear appreciation of the specific principles that gave us liberty upon which to evaluate the inferiority of conflicting principles also presented in the classroom. Failure at this point in the last sixty years, be it excused in the name of academic freedom or emancipation of the mind, or what have you, is a scandalous treachery to liberty. In a world where practicing political and moral principles makes the difference between liberty and despotism, failure-to teach them comprehensively, pointedly, and positively with scholarly competence and intellectual honesty serves the interest of those who would enslave us. Failing to implant or inculcate these principles of our founding is a tyranny of the mind that deprives students of the basis for their freedom of choice. In their citizenship, students cannot hope to choose soundly between alternatives they do not know and understand clearly. Some liberate and stimulate people to be responsible; other alternatives cause men's character to ebb and lead to socialism.

The preamble to the University of Virginia's policy resolution of 1825 reads as follows: "Whereas it is the duty of this board to the government (of the United States) under which it lives, and especially to that (of Virginia) of which this University is the immediate creation, to pay especial attention to the principles of government which shall be inculcated therein, and to provide that none shall be inculcated which are incompatible with those on which the Constitutions of this state, and of the United States were genuinely based in the common opinion: and for this purpose it may be necessary to point out specifically where these principles are to be found legitimately developed . . ."

The resolution went on to specify six writings that in the board's opinion reflected the unanimously supported distinct government principles unique to America and upon which youth should be indoctrinated. Two of the documents were of an expository nature known for the clarity in which the ideals of government are amplified and their practical benefits applied to human nature. They were: John Locke's *Essay Concerning the True Original Extent and End of Civil Government* (published in 1690) and Algernon Sidney's *Discourses Concerning Government* (1698).

The first four documents referred to were: The Declaration of Independence; Washington's Farewell Address; the Virginia Resolutions of 1799 (adopted by the Virginia Legislature); and the *Federalist* (papers).[4] These were listed in that resolution as being sound sources of "the general principles of liberty and rights of man in nature and society."

---

[4] Hamilton Albert Long, *Your American Yardstick* (Philadelphia Heritage Books, 1963), pp. 141-3.

The effect of the obscurity in which these key documents have been held over the past sixty years is only too apparent. Of this edifice of human strength or unique principles needed in order to be free and independent of the "entanglements" of "bountiful philosophy," George Washington in his Farewell Address said, ". . . it is easy to foresee that . . . from different quarters, such pains will be taken, many artifices employed, to weaken in your minds the conviction of this truth . . ."

There is considerable evidence that contention among religious groups trying to impose their sectarian doctrine through public education was used to confound the religious people so that the educators and cultural leaders who wanted God removed from education could do it completely. Instead of contending with each other, believers in the God of creation mentioned in the Declaration of Independence should unify on this point and encourage the re-instatement of the knowledge of the non-sectarian Creator and Judge of nations.

America is a melting pot for people from all over the world who come to escape persecution and share in our abundance. Most come with a respect and awe for our freedom and the God of our fathers. Our religions are Protestant, Catholic, Jewish and many others. We need to unify on the general point, however, of supporting one nation under God.

This is consistent with the Christian impetus that shaped America.

The responsibility of government education is to be consistent with its basis of existence and enhance the atmosphere for belief and trust in God the Provider and Judge, while avoiding specific sectarian emphasis. A chief tenent of Christianity, for instance, is that all men are equal before God and their acceptance or rejection of Christ is voluntary and a personal responsibility, not a matter for government dictation. Men are responsible and must choose and chart their own lives, including their sectarian choice of a religion.

There is a place where we should stand without compromise for the sectarian doctrine of our specific religious persuasion and personal walk with God. This place is in the private sector as individuals. Here in the land of liberty, supported in a general way by the Creator-concept in education, each religion can give its testimony and seek the truth for personal salvation, spiritual growth, and a broader following in the private sector.

It is also important in analyzing this to see that quality humanities curriculum suffered much to foreign philosophies that were promoted in the teacher training colleges and hit the public schools almost simultaneously with some legitimate additions to education—home economics, clerical science, trades, etc. It is ironic that these legitimate improvements which made public education as an experience for youth almost life itself, made the removal of God and the positive emphasis of the unique principles of American government even more devastating.

People, including public school teachers, are voting by the thousands against state-controlled schools. They are doing it by taking their young out of public schools, placing them in private schools that support God and country. Millions will do it once they see what is going on.

NAST CARTOON—MODERN MEANING

Thomas Nast was credited by Lincoln as being a big asset in winning the Civil War. When General Grant was asked who was the foremost figure in civil life developed by the rebellion, he replied, "I think Thomas Nast. He did as much as any one man to preserve the Union and bring the war to an end."

After the war Nast turned to political cartoons, and it was his relentless pursuit of the Tweed Ring which was credited with the final overthrow of that cynical pack of municipal pirates.

Best known of all Nast's cartoons was "The Tammany Tiger Loose" (1877) in the arena, devouring law and justice as Boss Tweed and his associates look on. As much as any single influence, this cartoon galvanized the forces of decency that toppled the rotten structure of the plunderbound.

Placards have been placed above Nast's "Tammany Tiger" (see sketch) to depict some of the ethically nihilistic philosophy fostered in American education since the early 1900's.

The elitist professionals, the tyrants of the mind, who would replace traditional education and cultural emphasis upon which individual liberty rests, are in the bleachers. In the arena are the victims: our daughters, our sons, and our national strength.

CHAPTER 6

A Judge's Viewpoint:
America's Next Chapter[1]

Almost every day in America there are distinguished citizens speaking out in protest of the direction toward socialism our country is taking. These speeches are not reported in the nation's press, nor on radio or television, in most instances. Yet, the crescendo of voices from the people is rising and the voice of the everyday, honest, sincere taxpaying citizen of this country needs to be heard. It is one voice that makes sense in today's world.

Such a voice was that of the Honorable Kermit V. Rooke, judge of the juvenile and domestic relations district court in the city of Richmond, Virginia. His speech was delivered in the Spring of 1975 and he called it "The Next Chapter in the History of America." He said:

"I want to talk with you about a book which is now being written. It is a story in which all of us here are personally involved, a drama in which each of us has a role to play. I want to talk about the next chapter in the History of America.

". . . . As is proper, we . . . review the pages and the events of

1 George S. Benson, from "The War Has Begun," *National Program*, December, 1975, pp. 3-4.

our history, enjoying the satisfaction and sensing the pride which are justified by the beautiful and glorious story of America, from its beginning. . . .

"We . . . honor and pay tribute to our forefathers, their courage and their strength, their devotion and their love of independence and freedom.

We presume here to discuss this next episode of our history not as a literary or intelligent exercise, but in the hope that someone listening, or perhaps all of us together, may be able to influence the way the story is to go.

"Let us begin with a problem with which I am familiar, the matter of crime. How will this problem look in retrospect? How important will it be as our history continues to develop? Crime in America has more than doubled in the past ten years. Throughout our beloved America there is a spreading wave of disrespect for the law, for life, for security in our homes, a destructive malignancy eating away upon the right of Americans to be free and to live in peace.

"The Attorney General of the United States, the top law-enforcement official of our nation, maintains an efficient and expensive network of sources of information and statistics on crime. The current Attorney General, and the one who preceded him in that office, both have publicly stated that, with the existing rate of increase in crime, *our nation cannot survive ten more years*. Hence, unless we are prepared to disprove these opinions we must assume that our next chapter is the end of the book, that it will be a short chapter, and at its end a great Nation will die.

"In respect to this problem, I suggest that little effort has been made in recent years to avert this tragic end to our history. We have made heroes of criminals. We have made crime easy and profitable, statistically involving less risk than legitimate investments. A recent survey in which I have confidence reveals that 66 percent of the crimes committed in this country are never reported to the police, because our people have reached the conclusion that it isn't worth the trouble. The survey continues that of those reported, arrested and convicted, less than two percent ever spend as much as one day in jail. Is it to be our national policy, the will of Americans, to surrender in these circumstances, or must we, with

God's help, dedicate ourselves to changing the course of history? Think about it.

"These are other problems which cast a disturbing shadow over the future of America, as we meditate about the next chapter of its history. A problem of major significance is the quality of public officials, the character of those to whom we entrust the management of our country. Previous chapters tell us that in the formative years of our national development we were blessed with honest, dedicated, courageous men in the higher offices of our central government. America did not blossom forth, as a mythological Phoenix, great and powerful at the moment of its birth two hundred years ago. It grew and prospered because it was blessed with the leadership of good men, honest, courageous men who, as they stated when they declared their independence, pledged their lives, their fortunes and their sacred honor. But now we must state that men of this kind and quality have been succeeded in the main, by politicians who have lost and betrayed the confidence of most Americans, and forfeited the trust of most of the rest of the world. Statesmen have degenerated to politicians, of both political parties, whose stock explanation of every failure is to blame the other political party: by politicians who cater to irresponsiblilty of the unproductive, enticing their votes by dangling before them a slice of the heart of a dying nation. If leadership of this kind and character, who survive politically through subsidizing failure and penalizing success, continues to write the script of our history, may God forgive us all for the next chapter of the history of America.

"We should ponder too, as to what the next episode of this drama will reflect respecting the financial affairs of our nation. Our central government now owes approximately 500 billion dollars. It began its current year of operation with a budget indicating a deficit of $69 billion. That is to say, our Federal Government proposes to spend $69 billion more than the most optimistic estimate of its income. Twenty years ago the total budget was by chance about equal to this year's expected deficit. This year the total budget is 367 billion dollars, 69 billion over estimated income. This, to state it plainly, can only be described as total, disgraceful, shameless irresponsibility, draining the last of life's blood from America. We should ponder how this will develop in the next chapter.

". . . Let me humbly suggest, also, that America survived the ordeals of its infancy, and grew and prospered when its leaders and its people recognized the true and only source of their blessings. They directed their supplications and their praise, not to Washington, D.C., or to politicians, but to the Supreme Master of us all. The proud history of our Nation, its success and its beauty, reflects nothing so clearly as the fact that its leadership and its people deserved to be sustained by the divine will of God. If the chapter we now compose is the final chapter, if the story ends in failure, chaos, and destruction, this too will reflect His will.

"Let us now reflect upon the fact that the script for the next performance has not been written, in its final form, and there is yet a little time for us to have a part in its composition.

"First, let us make it clear to those who lead us and to those who aspire to be our leaders that we will not surrender America to criminals and others who manifest disrespect for the rules by which we live, the Constitution and the law. Hear us clearly when we say that the sociologists and bleeding hearts have had their day and they have struck out. We want them off the payroll and out of the picture.

"Second, let us clarify the distinction between the statesmen and politicans. Those who would lead us now take note that America is fed up with politics and politicians, that the device of both political parties of blaming gross and growing failures upon the opposite party is a plain, transparent shame and we want these creatures out of our lives. They disgrace the memory of statesmen and defile the pages of our history.

"Third, let us announce in clear and convincing language that a central government which squanders tax money as is now being done, is irresponsible, inexcusable, bordering, in our judgment, very closely upon a criminal fraud upon those who produce the revenue and pay the bills of America. Let us challenge those who question that this is our view to submit to us a constitutional amendment requiring a balanced budget and the orderly reduction of our national debt.

"Fourth, let us reduce the term of office of all judges, and make it clear to all others who are paid by public taxation that they are the servants of those who sustain them and accountable to the sovereign will of the people of America.

"Fifth, let us make it very clear that the national fiscal policy of penalizing the success of those who produce and subsidizing the failures of those who do not produce is contrary to the national will and must be stopped.

"Finally, and most profoundly, let each one of us closely examine our own lives, thinking clearly and speaking plainly, remembering that our future and the destiny of our Nation must conform to the will of the Master. He will decide how we deserve the chapter to be written and when and how the story will end."

CHAPTER 7

Solzhenitsyn's Viewpoint:
Better Dead than a Scoundrel[1]

My warnings, the warnings of others—Sakharov's very grave warning directly from the Soviet Union, these warnings go unheeded. Most of them fall, as it were, on the ears of the deaf—people who do not want to hear them.

Once I used to hope that experience of life could be handed on, nation to nation, and from one person to another. But now I am beginning to have doubts about this. Perhaps everyone is fated to live through every experience himself in order to understand.

In actual fact, our Russian experience is vitally important to the West because, by some chance of history, we have trodden the path the West is taking 70 or 80 years before the West. And, now it is a rather strange sensation that we look at what is happening to you when many social phenomena are repeating what happened in Russia before it collapsed. Our experience of life is of vital importance to the West but I

1 *Third Century Report*, April 15, 1976, pp. 5-6, Michael Charlton interview British Broadcasting Corp., March 1, 1976, aired in U.S. by Wm. Buckley "Firing Line."

"One of the most important pieces of journalism ever." *Wall Street Journal*

am not convinced that you are capable of assimilating it
without having gone through it right to the end yourselves.

*One could cite many examples . . . a certain retreat by the
older generation, yielding their intellectual leadership to the
younger generation. It is against the natural order of things
for those who are youngest, with the least experience of life,
to have the greatest influence in directing the life of society.*

*One can say, then, this is what forms the spirit of the age,
this current of public opinion, when people in authority—
well-known professors, scientists—are reluctant to enter into
an argument even when they hold a different opinion.*

*And so, there is a certain abdication of responsibility
which is typical here where there is complete freedom. While
enjoying such great freedom, the journalists and writers lose
their sense of responsibility before history, before their own
people.*

Then there is now this universal education of revolutionaries, the more so the more extreme they are! Similarly, before the Revolution, we had in Russia if not a cult of terror
in society then a fierce defense of the terrorists. People in
good positions, intellectuals, professors, liberals spent a great
deal of effort, anger and indignation in defending terrorists.
The press does not feel responsibility for its judgements. It
makes judgements and sticks on labels with the greatest of
ease. Mediocre journalists simply make headlines of their
conclusions which suddenly become the general opinion
throughout the West.

Take the word "nationalist". It has become almost mean-
ingless. If someone suggests that his country should have a
large army, conquer the countries which surround it, should
go on expanding its empire, that sort of person is a nationalist.

But if, on the contrary, I suggest that my country should
free all the people it has conquered, should disband the army,
should stop all aggressive actions—who am I? A nationalist!

If you love England what are you? A nationalist! And,
when are you not a nationalist? When you hate England,
then you are not a nationalist.

". . . . possessing freedom, not to value it"

I am not a critic of the West. I am a critic of the weakness

of the West. I am a critic of a fact, which we can't compre-
hend: how can one lose one's spiritual strength, one's will-
power, and possessing freedom not to value it? Not to be
willing to make sacrifices for it?

"Which way is the West going?"

. . . two years ago and three years ago . . . the Soviet leadership was experiencing so many difficulties, so many failures,
that it had to seek some way out. Indeed, I thought that the
way out was to seek the path of evolution—certainly not the
revolutionary path. Not an explosion . . . an evolutionary,
smooth path which would offer a way out of this terrible system.

*However, today all these suggested solutions have lost
their practical value. Over the last two years terrible things
have happened. The West has given up not only four-five-or-
six countries, the West has given up all its world positions.
The West has given everything away so impetuously, has
done so much to strengthen the tyranny in our country, that
today all these questions are no longer relevant in the Soviet
Union.*

Opposition has remained but I have already said many
times that our movements of opposition and spiritual revival,
like any spiritual process, is a slow process. But your capitulations, like all political processes, move very quickly. The
speed of your capitulations has so rapidly overtaken the
pace of our moral regeneration that at the moment the Soviet
Union can only move along one path: the flourishing of totalitarianism.

. . . it would be more appropriate . . . if I were to ask you
which way the West is going? Because at the moment the
question is not how the Soviet Union will find a way out of
totalitarianism but how the West will be able to avoid the
same fate.

How will the West be able to withstand the unprecedented
force of totalitarianism? That is the problem.

"Irreconcilable Contradiction"

My outlook on life has been formed largely in concentra-
tion camps—that part of my life which is reflected in the
'Gulag Archipelago.' I don't know whether western listeners

would find my words embarrassing. It is difficult for me to judge this kind of reaction. But, I would put it like this:

Those people who have lived in the most terrible conditions, on the frontier between life and death—be it people from the West or from the East, they all understand that between good and evil there is an irreconcilable contradiction: that it is not one and the same thing—good and evil. That one cannot build one's life without regard to this distinction.

I am surprised that pragmatic philosophy consistently scorns moral considerations; and, nowadays in the Western press, we read a candid declaration of the principle that moral considerations have nothing to do with politics; they do not apply and should not, so to speak, be applied.

I would remind you that in 1939 England thought differently. If moral considerations were not applicable to politics then it would have been quite incomprehensive why on earth England went to war with Hitler's Germany. *Pragmatically*, you could have got out of the situation. But, England chose the moral course and experienced and demonstrated to the world perhaps the most brilliant and heroic period in its history.

But today we have forgotten this. Today the English political leaders state quite frankly that they not only recognize *any* power over *any* territory regardless of its moral character but they even hasten to recognize it—even try to be the first to do so.

Tyrants, bandits, puppets have come to power and pragmatic philosophy says: That doesn't matter, we have to recognize them.

. . . one should not consider that the great principles of freedom finish at your own frontiers; that as long as you have freedom let the rest have pragmatism. No! Freedom is indivisible and one has to take a moral attitude toward it.

"On the verge of collapse"

I wouldn't be surprised at the sudden and imminent fall of the West. (including America)

I would like to make myself clear. The situation at the moment is such, the Soviet Union's economy is on such a war footing, that even if it were the *unanimous* opinion of all its members of the Politbureau not to start a war this would no

longer be in their power. To avoid this would require an ago-
nizing change from a monstrous war economy to a normal
peace economy.

The situation now is such that one must not think of what
might happen unexpectedly in the West. The West is on the
verge of collapse created by its own hands.

*The most important aspect of detente today is that there is
no ideological detente. You western people, you simply can't
grasp the power of Soviet propaganda.*

To remove this crust (of detente) will take only one morning; *one single morning.* You can't be turned away from detente so simply. To turn you away from your present position
one would need a year or two. But, in the Soviet Union, *one
morning—one command—is enough!*

*One can't raise the question of detente without ideological
detente. If you are hated and hounded throughout the press,
in every single lecture—what sort of detente is that? You are
shown up as villains who can be tolerated—well, maybe—for
one more day. This is not detente.*

As for the spirit of Helsinki, may I ask a question in my
turn? How do you explain that, for instance, over the last few
months there has been hardly any news coming out of the Soviet Union of the continuing persecution of dissidents? If
you will forgive me I will answer this myself: *the journalists
have bowed to the spirit of Helsinki.* I know for a fact that
western journalists in Moscow, who have been given the right
of freer movement, in return for this and in the spirit of Helsinki, no longer accept information about any new persecu-
tions of dissidents in the Soviet Union.

"A terrible thought"

It is the import of technology which is saving the Soviet
Union. That's true.

But, I return to that terrible statement of Bertrand Russell.
I don't understand at all why Bertrand Russell said, "Better
red than dead." Why did he not say it would be better to be
brown than dead? There is no difference.

All my life, and the life of my generation, the life of those
who share my views, we all have one standpoint:
Better to be dead than a scoundrel.

In this horrible expression of Bertrand Russell there is an

absence of all moral criteria. Looked at it from a short distance these words allow one to maneuver and to continue to enjoy life. But, from a long-term point of view, it will undoubtedly destroy those people who think like that. It is a terrible thought.

Detente is necessary, but detente with open hands. Show that there is no stone in the hands! But, your partners, with whom you are conducting detente, have a stone in their hands and it is so heavy that it could kill you with one single blow.

Detente becomes self-deception, that's what it's all about. Nuclear war is not even necessary to the Soviet Union. You can be taken simply with bare hands. Why on earth then should one have nuclear war? If you are raising your hands and are giving in, why have a nuclear war? They can take you simply like that without nuclear war.

CHAPTER 8

An Immigrant's Viewpoint: The America We Lost[1]

When I first came to America, forty-four years ago, I learned a new meaning of the word "Liberty"—freedom from government.

I did not learn a new meaning for "democracy." The European country from which I came, Italy, was at that time as "democratic" as America. It was a constitutional monarchy, with a parliament, free and frequent elections, lots of political parties and plenty of freedom of religion, speech, press and assembly.

But my native country was government-ridden. A vast bureaucracy held it in its countless tentacles. Regardless of the party or coalition of parties that might be in power at the moment, the government was everywhere. Wherever one looked, one saw signs of the ever-present government—in the uniforms of numberless royal, rural and municipal policemen, soldiers, officers, bold-braided functionaries of all sorts. You could not take a step without government intervention.

Many industries and businesses were government-owned and government-run—railroads, telegraphs, salt and tobacco

1 Mario A. Pei, "The America We Lost" Foundation of Economic Education's "Clipping of Note" No. 51.

among them. No agreement, however trivial, was legal unless written on government-stamped paper. If you stepped out of the city into the country and came back with a ham, a loaf of bread or a bottle of wine, you had to stop at the internal-revenue barriers and pay duty to the government, and so did the farmers who brought in the city's food supply every morning. No business could be started or run without the official sanction of a hundred bureaucrats.

Young people did not dream of going into business for themselves; they dreamed of a modest but safe government job, where they would have tenure, security and a pitiful pension at the end of their plodding careers. There was grinding taxation to support the many government functions and the innumerable public servants. Everybody hated the government—not just the party in power, but the government itself. They had even coined a phrase, "It's raining—thief of a government!" as though even the evils of nature were the government's fault. Yet, I repeat, the country was democratically run, with all the trappings of a many-party system and all the freedoms of which we in America boast today.

America in those days made you open your lungs wide and inhale great gulps of freedom-laden air, for here was one additional freedom—freedom from government.

The Government was conspicuous by its very absence. There were no men in uniform, save occasional cops and firemen, no visible bureaucrats, no stifling restrictions, no Government monopolies. It was wonderful to get used to the American system: To learn that a contract was valid if written on the side of a house; that you could move not only from the city to the country but from state to state and never be asked what your business was or whether you had anything to declare; that you could open and conduct your own business, provided it was a legitimate one, without Government interference; that you could go from one end of the year to the other and never have contact with the national Government, save the cheery postman who delivered your mail with a speed and efficiency unknown today; that there were no national taxes, save hidden excises and import duties that you did not even know you paid.

In that horse-and-buggy America, if you made an honest dollar, you could pocket it or spend it without having to figure what portion of it you "owed" the Government or what possible deductions you could allege against that Government's claims. You did not have to keep books and records of every bit of income and expenditure or run the risk of being called a liar and a cheat by someone in authority.

Above all, the national ideal was not the obscure security of a Government job, but the boundless opportunity that all Americans seemed to consider their birthright. Those same Americans loved their Government then. It was there to help, protect and defend them, not to restrict, befuddle and harass them. At the same time, they did not look to the Government for a livelihood or for special privileges and handouts. They were independent men in the full sense of the word.

Foreign-born citizens have been watching with alarm the gradual Europeanization of America over the past twenty years. They have seen the growth of the familiar European-style Government octopus, along with the vanishing of the American spirit of freedom and opportunity and its replacement by a breathless search for "security" that is doomed to defeat in advance in a world where nothing, not even life itself, is secure.

Far more than the native-born, they are in a position to make comparisons. They see that America is fast becoming a nineteenth-century-model European country. They are asked to believe that this is progress. But they know from bitter experience that it just isn't so.

CHAPTER 9

A Humanities Chairman's Viewpoint: Can Integrity Be Restored?[1]

The great question on this sorry eve of our second centennial is this:

"How can integrity be restored—indeed: Can integrity be restored?"

There are those who prescribe more schools, more education. To this I say, *Hogwash!* We are up to here in education and got ourselves into this mess. No, ours is not a shortage of *brains,* but a shortage of *integrity.* Our problem is not one of *knowledge* but one of *morality.* The most embarrassing human fact I know this late in the twentieth century is that we have human knowledge enough and to spare to solve nearly all of our social problems but we lack the gut-level goodness to use our wisdom that way. Take the population explosion. I sometimes say facetiously to my students, "This is a very promising problem for after all we do know what's causing it!" I mean that we have the facts, we have the knowledge, but we lack the values to use them rightly.

1 George E. LaMore, Jr., "A Bicentennial Briefing," *Farm and Land* •
Realtor, November, 1975, pp. 9-11.

This is one thing that worries me so much about many of my younger friends. As new fads and leaders arise they don't seem to ask of them: "Does this make sense? Does this add up?" Instead they seem to ask the romantic questions, "Does this grab you? Does this turn you on? Does it have the right vibes—ring your bell?" When the charismatic leader arises, believe me, he will have all these things going for him, and in a week or ten days you will be goose stepping to ideals you never intended in the first place.

Self-Discipline

Thus there are certain qualities which I insist on in any new leaders or groups of leaders from whatever generation. The first of these qualities is self-discipline. You cannot master the world until you first master yourself. You have to become the first citizens of the kind of world you say you want. Too many cases of our so-called new leaders practice the private morality of alley cats and the corporate morality of the jungle, and you know how long a society based on such values would last.

What do we blame

Too many of our leaders practice what I call the New Astrology. In the old astrology you put the blame for things on the stars. Why the stars? When passing the buck it is well to pass it as far as possible, and the stars are the furthest thing we know. In the new astrology, we do not assign blame to the stars. Instead we blame everything on other nebulous bodies—"the establishment, the system, the organization," but never on ourselves. Yet, until we change ourselves we have changed nothing. Mohandas Gandhi was a social reformer, clearly aware of the changes necessary in the political system, yet his creed throughout his life ran, "Turn the search light inward." Master the self.

Hippies, Puritans and change

One of the embarrasing facts I have come to conclude about history is one not likely to endear me to the present
• generation of students: History is never changed by the Hippies but only by the Puritans, the self-disciplined Puritans,

whether they be the Puritans of Maoist China, early Massachusetts or the first Methodists. The first quality I must discern in true leadership is self-discipline.

Sense of history

And the second quality I insist on is what I call a sense of history. By this I mean an awareness of how the game has gone so far, not that tomorrow's game will repeat yesterday's, but it will have a family resemblance. Too many of the revolutionary leaders of modern time have had it as their basic strategy to "break with the past and start fresh." Well, when you break with the past you just start over again from scratch, repeating all the blunders already contained in the history books you burned so you could tell your lies retroactively. For me, progress does not come from breaking with the past but from building upon the best of the past, and to do that you have to know it.

Humility

The third quality I seek in any authentic leader is humility. By humility I mean the capacity to hear other voices besides one's own. Too many of the shrill leaders in modern demonstrations in universities have sought to boo down, shout down or even shoot down anybody with an alternative voice. This is tragic!

By humility I mean the capacity to listen as well as to speak—the capacity to learn as well as to teach. By humility I mean the capacity to face one's faults before one's faults prove fatal. I guess that phrase could stand as the ultimate commentary on all that we have learned about Watergate and the arrogance of power up to this point.

Too many leaders have had the notion that Truth comes in the form of a solo, and they must get everybody to sing the same tune. I believe that human truth comes not in the form of a solo but in the form of a chorus of many voices, and the authentic role of the leader is not to get everybody to sing the same tune but to find the harmonies possible among the voices and even do creative things with the dissonances.

When we have restored in our leaders and ourselves this basic integrity which is self-disciplined, aware of history and creatively humble then we shall again have a sense of identity—who we really are and where we are going. The great English scholar C.S. Lewis once asked, "How can we see God face to face until we have faces?" That is the heart of the matter. Too many theological writers have suggested that it is God who is anonymous and faceless. No. It is we who have lost our identity and we must find it again.

Goodness is no longer optional

Deep down in the American mind it seems to me there has always been a subtle, Satanic notion. We may have attended church, paid dues and sung hymns, but we have harbored the notion that goodness is a kind of optional luxury item. You can be as selfish and unscrupulous as you want, and as long as you make your pile and don't get caught you are a success. Now we are at the end of that myth. In a time when six men in a single atomic bomber carry more destructive force than all the bombs dropped by both sides in World War II, goodness is not optional but the quintessential ingredient for our survival.

Just now in Central Missouri there are some one hundred fifty rockets lined up, any one of which can strike Moscow in twenty minutes with a force fifty times greater than the weapons dropped on Hiroshima. Goodness in a world like this is not luxury. We are literally boxed into the need for goodness. But when goodness arises out of desperation rather than faith it is questionable whether it can be trusted in the long haul. It can be as impermanent as fox hole religion. Whatever the liabilities, we are literally being called upon to be the best of people in the worst of times, and any lesser challenge is a bluff.

Leadership

But supposing integrity could be restored to persons and government, would this be enough? My answer is No, not quite. Integrity is a quiet goodness, goodness with its motor idling, goodness going nowhere. No, in addition to integrity there must be a sense of direction—leadership. But here our crisis is acute.

We are passing through what has been called a crisis of authority—we do not trust our leaders and with good cause. The twentieth century has literally been a Zoo Parade of messianic leaders who have promised perfection and led man to the brink of perdition. Now we trust almost nobody, so say the scholars.

Actually things are a bit more subtle. It is true that many persons are saying, "I trusted this cause, I trusted that cause, none of them worked, I'll trust nobody after this." They cop out, becoming dogmatic doubters and cynics.

Follow anything that moves?

On the other hand, as Dostoyevski once put it, "Man is a creature who has to live for something," and when man is desperate enough for something to live for he is liable to follow almost anything that moves. This is the phenomenon that worries me most. There is no other way of explaining the way in which man has followed the most insane messiahs and fads up to the present time.

Alfred Korscybski has suggested that there are seasons when mankind seems strangely divided between those who believe too little and those who believe too much—the cynics and the fanatics.

For me, some of the most fateful words of our century are not liable to grab you until I tell you who said them. The words are "The capacity of modern man to believe is almost unbelievable." The author? Mussolini, and he should know, for it is almost unbelievable that modern, sophisticated man could have fallen for that tub of lard and sworn, "Il Duce can do no wrong!" But he did for he was desperate for something to live for.

Charismatic leaders

I fear that we are in a season when charismatic leaders are liable to start coming out of the woodwork making wild promises to the desperate. By charismatic leaders I mean those who have amazing power to electrify and motivate others.

Of course not all charisma is evil; some is good. There are charismatic leaders who come wrapped in a white sheet like Gandhi and those who come wrapped in a red flag like

Lenin. There are charismatic leaders who come wearing the sandals of peace and those who come wearing the hobnail boots of war.

The longer I study the role of charismatic leaders the more I see that their success largely depends upon their arising in what I call a charismatic situation. A charismatic situation always has two components.

They are: a vacuum of leadership and a romantically motivated populace. Into the vacuum of leadership steps the new messiah making impossible promises, and for a reason people longing for the light will follow him. By a romantic populace I mean people who do not respond with their heads but with their hearts.

Living in the meantime

We are living in a strange between-the-times season of history. In the words of Matthew Arnold, "The old world with its confidences is dead, and the new world seems powerless to be born." We are living in the meantime, and a very mean time it is. Yet it is in seasons like this that there sometimes arises in societies a renewing grace. This grace that renews men and societies seldom arises in man's seasons of confidence and arrogance, but in his seasons of confession and humility, and certainly we are in such a season when our Congress went on record this past year favoring without a dissenting vote a national day of Humiliation, Fasting and Prayer.

If you believe this possibility of renewal, then you understand the central strategy of the greatest commencement address ever given. It was not given at any college or university but on a rural hillside in Galilee two thousand years ago. The basic idea was this: New life cannot arise in us until we first admit our sickness for only then can we be healed. Blessed are we when we admit our emptiness; only then can we be filled.

This is the only hope that I can hold before you on this eve of our nation's bicentennial, and you may want to respond: That's a mighty sober hope! And you are right, but the longer I live the more I am convinced that sober hope is the only kind of hope man ever could trust. Thus I wish for us this powerful renewal, and I wish for our nation a blessed birthday, and I have spoken the way I have because I am persuaded that these two events depend terribly much on each other.

CHAPTER 10

A Grand Jury's Viewpoint: Problems in Education[1]

The recent murder of a (local university) co-ed and frequent reports of student radicals and other activists using campus media to pulpiteer, sensationalize and otherwise promote illicit sex, drug abuse, draft evasion, defamation of our country and our leaders demands the attention of this report.

DR. CLARK KERR'S ESTIMATE

Perhaps the common motivating force which gives national and international direction is best described by Dr. Clark Kerr, former President of Berkeley; in a message to alumni (from *California Monthly*, February 1965).

"The United States is now a nation of young people; about 46 percent of the population is under 25 years of age. Nearly

[1] Extracts, Grand Jury Presentment, pp. 1-15.

Extracts from 11th Judicial District of Iowa
Story County Grand Jury Presentment.
Problems in Education
Dated: December 23, 1968

five million of these young people are now in college. This leads a few of the activists to have a sense of potential power and a desire for actual power—power certainly against the college or university administration; potentially against the faculty, and particularly against society at large. There is a new drive in the minds of some student activists; they see themselves as new men of power working in a nerve center of society."

POWER TO CAPTURE YOUTH THROUGH INDOCTRINATION

For many years psychologists and educators have recognized the processes by which thought and behavioral patterns acquired in youth become the basis for adult motivation. In modern times thoughtful observers have become progressively aware that moral, social, and political concepts implanted during the time of mental immaturity not only participate in the conduct of later life, but, once acquired, such concepts become dominant and often unalterable in the adult. Thus, captive audiences of immature minds provide powerful and much prized forums for ideological indoctrination.

Knowledge itself is not necessarily wisdom. Many radical leaders are highly educated. Castro with a Juris Doctorate Degree is an example of such a man.

PURPOSE AND EXTENT OF REPORT

Our goal in general was to try to understand what is happening and from these observations suggest or make constructive recommendations that may be useful in improving education.

CONCLUSIONS OF THE GRAND JURY

The concrete evidence of failures educationally and administratively in the humanities is well illustrated by a quotation in the *Des Moines Sunday Register*, June 7, 1967. According to the article the *New York Times* had asked an Iowa State student, where he picked up his radical ideas. The article referred to a teacher by name . . . and concluded, "He was a history teacher here two years ago. I took a course in Ideas of Western Civilization from him. That got me started."

There doesn't seem to be any doubt that some teachers are guilty of using their status to effectively subvert or undermine the morals and allegiance of some students.

THE CAUSE

Our investigation indicates that the main reason for the youthful rebellion, attitude of carelessness in their morals, proneness to anarchy, and the so-called generation gap, is the loss of confidence of the young in the wisdom embedded in their heritage. This wedge being in proportion to:

(1) Education—impotency in communicating established knowledge in the humanities. Failure to clearly implant these truths detaches future generations from past experience—the very basis of education in the humanities.

We should not proceed as though the wisdom of our fathers were too tentative to serve as an educational base.

In the field of morality all basic truths have been apprehended. All the changing conditions we hear so much about do not affect the validity or applicability of the central directives of human conduct. These truths are demonstrable in terms of benefits and as to how it is that those who disregard them fall easily into alien pitfalls of facism, lawlessness, drug addiction, etc. There is no greater contribution a teaching institution can make to human progress and purpose than to endow students at all levels with this knowledge. All other aspects of education ought to be subservient.

(2) The ascendancy to influential positions of radicals who encourage neutral or impotent education on our part and fill this vacuum with their . . . approach of distrust and violent revolution, and the propaganda that the good things we want can be obtained thereby.

After making our observations we analyzed four identifiable characteristics of the radical phenomenon. These groups all fall below what the general public, in our opinion, expects and has a right to expect of the teachers they hire and policy in public education. These groups are discussed in detail in this report but briefly, (I) their goal, destroy the present system and (II) take control, by tactics through (III) dishonesty of various forms, and (IV) militant aggressiveness.

PUBLIC CONCERN

Many complaints are made to the university and the regents not only about the conspicuous public eruptions, but the quiet activity of the radicals as well. This includes mature taxpayers in general, parents, legislators and fellow faculty members.

The people, including the grass-roots level of our society, ... are greatly concerned in the opinion of this Grand Jury.

The public importance of our youth coming to maturity thoroughly indoctrinated in human nature is because they are the voters of tomorrow. Is not the best future government that one which is the best reflection of human nature? If men were angels, no government would be necessary.

Law enforcement of the university is remarkably good. Those who place their present faith and future hope in law enforcement to conduct humanity to brighter times, ignore, however, a fundamental psychological truth. Legal and material attempts to correct human conduct resulting from improper training must all end in failure. It is impossible to superimpose an effective code of ethics through compulsion. Police force provides nothing more corrective than temporary control of faulty behavior traceable to education's failure to implant established knowledge on morality and the precepts of individual responsibility in the educated.

Lincoln said 130 years ago, "If destruction be our lot, we must ourselves be its author and finisher. As a nation of free men, we must live through all time, or die by suicide."

WHERE TO GO FOR THE SOLUTION

The frustrating inability of the public to correct the distortion of academic freedom is due, in the Grand Jury's view, to the failure of the people to see the continuation of the atrocious abuses by radicals as a breakdown in the responsibility-authority principle that it really is! All organization, educational or otherwise, is an attempt at cooperation. Cooperation is not possible unless responsibility and authority go hand-in-hand.

The parents and taxpayers delegated their responsibility-authority powers indirectly through a chain of command selection of people who want to teach and agree with public policy.

The system of organization varies, but in Iowa the Board of Regents is responsible to the public for education at the state universities. It is at this level, the Board of Regents, where corrective policy must be laid down on behalf of the people.

If the problem is ever corrected by the public it will have to be at this level!

Two significant avenues in our political structure for corrective changes are the legislature and the governor. They have indirect responsibility because the people give the legislators control over appropriations and the governor controls the appointment of regents. Within the limits of the resources vested in them by the people they are in a position to encourage corrective changes.

The taxpayers, having the final responsibility for the universities, quite properly should have the authority to change the Board of Regents' membership or take other measures if they find themselves in disagreement with board policy. If the established procedures for government at this level leave the regents insensitive to the public interest, then it is time to update government through the established procedures.

Discretion in exercising authority, regardless of where vested, is assured. The public, having given the Board of Regents the responsibility to implement public policy, must leave them the authority to go to the university president who has the executive responsibility of the university. The university president, vested with the responsibility by the Board of Regents, has the authority to change his aides if he believes they are not carrying out his ideas, etc., on down the line.

MOST IMPORTANT EDUCATIONAL CHANGE NEEDED IN OUR VIEW

These suggestions relate to corrective measures in education in the humanities curriculum. In view of the Grand Jury, there need to be fundamental changes, not pressure to cover up the trouble.

1. Regents' policy changes which will sufficiently define and implement the elimination of moral pollution by faculty and paid speakers and will, "by all suitable means" . . . encourage "moral . . . improvement." Article IX, 2nd School . . . Sec. 3, Constitution, State of Iowa.

2. Need for increased emphasis at all levels of education on the American ideal. We referred briefly to this in the preface of this report, and we believe it needs reviewing almost weekly from the first grade through to maturity.

Our revolutionary concepts are a most exciting and important subject. Our soldier boys have been dying for this ideal. Education as never before should clearly teach it. Even in imperfection it has achieved greatness for Americans unparalleled in history.

It seems rather clear that the nerve center of society, the power for desirable social revolution, is inherent in the adult electorate rather than the schools, and that the radical pathfinders should be sent to the electorate, not to the captive audience of youthful minds.

The idea of radicals, that the people of this land should not be trusted with the complexities of education, is archaic. The very definition of practical greatness, which built America, entrusts the educational and political emphasis to the control of the people. This is a much safer place than providing a haven for radicals who are beyond responsibility to the public and emphasize what they want with impunity.

OBSERVATIONS IN THE PROBLEM AREA

At this point perhaps we should define to some extent what we mean in this report by radicals and militants in the context of their behavior as expressed by our interviews and investigation.

I. Their number one goal, both stated and apparent, is that they desire control of the useful university apparatus for a base to promote and direct their activities. There is no apparent limit! It seems to depend on just where they can get their hand in—classes, university news media, selection of guest speakers, extension outlets, etc.

One example of intrusion called to our attention—a citizen contacted a professor and suggested that the coming News Editors' Seminar might be informed by the university of a government pamphlet about the techniques of communist propaganda in the news media.

The citizen was told that it was not the business of the university to get involved in politics. The citizen was quite shocked to later read in the newspaper that an associate professor of history had lectured the editors on the possible future problem with certain local political groups.

II. General goal of destroying and tearing down. Radical salesmen appeal to idealistic students with words calculated to destroy the youthful faith in their heritage. The radicals have nothing to substitute except their control. Our problems are magnified by them but nothing is said about how these same problems fare in other countries, or how much more the minorities here have, for instance, compared to the majority in other parts of the world. Nothing is said of the great advances within and contributions to the world by our country! They are contemptuous of our President, major political parties, school administrations, existing rules, absolutes, established knowledge, etc. Much of the worst educational literature and speeches come to the students under the mantle of moral improvement.

These are quotations from one of a number of paid radical speakers.

Dick Gregory's speech at Iowa State University September 12, 1968: "I spend about 90% of my time now on college campuses . . ." Regarding LBJ: "I love to watch him on TV standing there drunk . . ." "This is the most morally polluted, insane nation on the face of this earth and it is your job to change it." "And I say to you youngsters in the process of trying to make this peacefully, orderly transition of bringing up the constitution over the capitalists, if they offer you too much resistance, then destroy them." "Let me tell you something, black folks used them two words, M—— F——. We used it a lot but we didn't invent it. White folks invented those two words, you just called it Oedipus Rex and dirty enough to teach world literature with it." ". . . Let's always remember that flag still ain't nothing but a rag, like all of the other flags on the face of this earth . . ."

This is not an isolated example but typical of much of the . . . approach we observed.

They deny the historic role of education which in part has been to pass on to maturing generations truths and experiences learned in the past, in order to avoid the mistakes of the past and better fulfill the dreams of tomorrow.

In place of established knowledge, they want relativism as the accepted educational premise.

Relativism for purposes of this discussion refers to the denial . . . of absolutes and puts evil on a par with discerned truth as a legitimate teaching subject. In the area of society and human nature such denial, when implemented, detaches future generations from past experience (oddly enough the very basis of education in the humanities).

Such foolishness gives a teaching license to those who promote illicit sex, use of decimating drugs, draft evasion, flag burning, etc., and places in question historically known good.

Such a position on fundamental tenets raises a very interesting question. If the desirability of sexual virtue and the undesirability of permitting over-night co-habitation in single student dorms is, as they say, a matter of opinion; if in fact sexual virtue and many other tenets such as basic honesty are not established knowledge suitable for classroom doctrine—what is the good of having humanities courses at all? When a radical teacher lectures, what is he accomplishing with the taxpayers' money? What is he accomplishing toward the encouragement of moral improvement?

III. Tactics used by radicals frequently disregard the minimum teacher standard of honesty. It is not unusual to hear them proclaim the virtues of equality and love, then extol violence, hatred and the use of harmful drugs in the same speech. In their effort to present a one-sided picture, they are even so bold as to suppress, if they can, opposing views. A notable and obvious example of this was the unsuccessful effort some time ago of a few staff members to stop the appearance of Herbert Philbrick as the speaker at the annual agriculture banquet.

One interviewee stated his concern relative to misrepresentations made . . . about our society. If students hear a lie often enough some begin to believe it!

The dishonest teacher represents a (bad) situation because in the class-room there is no easy way to detect and correct distortion until after it has adulterated young minds and even then it is sometimes hard to trace down and prove. Our observations are that frequently by then the radical has moved on to some other institution and is enjoying high academic standing teaching other young people.

Radicals making public speeches on the campus are much easier, of course, to detect but these even seem to get speaking engagements. It is interesting to note that these radicals charge our system with weakness when we apply some degree of selectivity at the educational level. Even with complete freedom they cannot sell their wonderful solution to the adult electorate. They subvert our political process and bypass the adult electorate and when they can get in the schools go to the captive audience of immature youth. Even there they employ deceptive tactics to sell their solution.

IV. Tactics aggressive, domineering and sometimes ruthless. In such cases the person with average interest and courtesy is no match. One of their tactics is rule by committee domination. They pressure administrators to relinquish their duty in a specific area and turn it over to a committee run perhaps by four staff and four students. In this way one radical professor who is willing to do a lot of hard work, and a radical student or two, pretty much administer according to their own interest. The most aggressive prevail over those teachers who feel obligated to spend their time teaching and learning rather than contending and squabbling over administrative detail.

The public manifestation of this aggressive characteristic is a matter of general news and on occasion involves open challenge of law.

OTHER OBSERVATIONS

Right of Taxpayer to Govern Challenged

Some deny the very right of the taxpayer electorate, who hire and pay teachers to assist in the education of their children, to govern educational policy.

Even though the parents and taxpayers hire a teacher, the . . . responsibility and authority originates and should remain with the parents and the taxpayers in general who pay the bill!

Further, looking at this we might ask—is it unreasonable to expect the Board of Regents through definitive delegation of responsibility to school executives to discontinue speakers who are liars, who blaspheme our flag, our heritage, or moral scruples on the grounds of academic freedom? Whose academic freedom—the parent-taxpayer or the radical teacher? Is the parent, who once had academic freedom, now to be deprived because of hiring a teacher? Most agree that anyone can teach what he pleases on his own responsibility, but not yield to his cry of academic freedom as he robs the taxpayers of their freedom to direct public education in the public interest based upon the learning process and established knowledge.

Church and State

A confusing point we have observed, which deserves special attention because it is prevalent among many citizens and is a handicap to good education, is an erroneous interpretation of separation of church and state. The principle does not mean that there is not to be an inter-mixing of people and ideas between church and state. Obviously, the mayor can be a church member and a school teacher can teach the established knowledge on morality. What it does mean is that there is to be a separation of powers of church, and of the state, over one another.

Some confuse teaching morality and its demonstrable values, which are legitimate and essential teaching matter in public schools, with denominational doctrines and forms of worship which some churches or atheistic religions may try to impose on schools and should not. The misunderstanding would give the erroneous impression that we must avoid teaching the established knowledge on morality in the state schools which happens to be shared or derived, for instance, from the Judeo-Christian beliefs.

A similarly confusing misconception regarding goals in morality is the erroneous assumption that since we can't all reach high goals of morality, we have no right to stress their desirability and importance when we teach.

Problems Feed Back and Compound If Not Corrected.

No single level of education can be considered in a vacuum, good or bad. It is going on! The students of colleges are, after all, the graduates of American elementary and secondary schools. We, the adults and teachers of today, are the graduates of high schools, colleges and universities in the recent past. Not only are various levels of American education interrelated, but the problems feed back upon one another to produce a complex of relationships which affect us all and must be realized. In the physical sciences a faulty practice may be found out in a matter of minutes or weeks. In professions such as medicine or architecture failures soon become apparent and are corrected. A faulty experiment with humanity is very dangerous because the whole society is involved and the error may not be detected for two or three generations and then be too late to reverse the impetus and avoid disaster. The highly educated Germany of recent times is an example of just such a disaster.

Home Failure

Although not a part of this study, it is recognized that lack of training in some homes is a serious and related problem—this accentuates the importance of good public education in the humanities which will salvage some home failures with its emphasis on established knowledge.

Under good public education you do not have maturing young people with good home training coming to school and losing faith in their heritage as it now happens.

CHAPTER 11

A Business Analyst's Viewpoint:
The Question of Liberty in America[1]

Over the next two decades, says Irving Kristol, American politics will be characterized by confrontation between the public sector, striving for control, and the private sector, struggling to retain its identity. Upon the outcome, Kristol believes, depends the continued existence of political freedom and personal liberty in America.

A native of New York City, where he still resides, Kristol has devoted a lifetime to the analysis of contemporary political thought.

He is a member of the National Council on the Humanities and a Fellow of the American Academy of Arts and Sciences. He is also a member of the Council on Foreign Relations.

In recent writings, Kristol has identified a "new class" of Americans who are bidding powerfully and successfully for control of the national economy. Large corporations are their favorite targets. But they are hostile to business in general, and, indeed, to the entire private sector. To explore this phe-

1 "The Question of Liberty in America," *CBMC Contact*, January-February, 1976, pp. 12-15. (Irving Kristol speaks)

nomenon. *Exxon USA* called on Professor Kristol. Our questions, and his answers, follow:

Q: Polls tell us public confidence in business is very low. If this is true, why do you suppose people are down on business?

KRISTOL: Polls can be misleading, and shouldn't always be taken at face value. Public confidence in *large corporations* is very low. But public confidence in business in general is actually fairly high. Ask Americans if they favor free enterprise and three out of four will say yes. But apparently many people see large corporations as distinct from the American tradition of free enterprise.

Q: Wasn't there a time when Americans thought better of large corporations?

KRISTOL: Not really. American public opinion has always been hostile to large enterprises. Size in business, in government, has always been feared and resented. Consider the vociferousness with which presidents such as Theodore Roosevelt and Woodrow Wilson attacked large corporations. But there was a brief period of about two decades when large corporations enjoyed a relatively good reputation. In the two decades from 1945 to 1965 people were recovering from the demoralizing effects of a severe depression and a world war. They wanted the things large corporations could give them: houses, cars, washing machines. But even more, the depression-scarred public wanted jobs with security and fringe benefits which large corporations could provide. So, there were about 20 years when large corporations were, on the whole, well regarded. But it's a mistake to view this as the norm. Polls reflect what amounts to a resumption of traditional attitudes toward big business.

Q: Who are the critics?

KRISTOL: In earlier times, criticism was largely confined to the radical left and the spokesmen for labor. Neither had much of a voice or influence. But today there is a new class hostile to business in general, and especially to large corporations. As a group, you find them mainly in the large and growing public sector and in the media. This new class consists of well educated and intelligent professionals who work in all levels of government: public officials, civil servants, bureaucrats; doctors, lawyers, and engineers in some form of public service; teachers and school administrators; psychologists, sociologists, and environmentalists; members of the media and more. No one knows how large this group is, but it could amount to as much as 15 percent of our population. These people are smart and articulate. They share a disinterest in personal wealth, a dislike for the free market economy, and a conviction that society may best be improved through greater governmental participation in the country's economic life. As a result of technological, economic, and social developments, this group has become terribly influential. They *are* the media. They *are* the educational system. Their dislike for the free market economy originates in their inability to exercise much influence over it so as to produce change. In its place they would prefer a system in which there is a very large political component. This is because the new class has a great deal of influence in politics. Thus, through politics, they can exercise a direct and immediate influence on the shape of our society.

Q: How much control does the new class want?

KRISTOL: That's not clear. They probably don't know. But they certainly want more. How much more will be determined by politics, and that is what politics is going to be about in the next 20 years.

Q: Do they want power for themselves?

KRISTOL: Oh, yes. A good example is environmentalism. Broadly interpreted, the environmental movement means the power to run the entire economy. What doesn't, in some way, affect the environment? Nothing people do is exempt, because everything we do affects the environment. So, if you interpret environmentalism literally, you are talking about giving power to a degree and of a sort that this country has never given to any class before.

Q: Do you mean personal power or governmental power?

KRISTOL: Both. After all, who runs the governmental agencies? Who works for HEW? Who staffs EPA? Agency staff people are prototypical members of the new class. More and more young lawyers, for example, choose a career in the public sector in preference to private practice. These are *the* typical representatives of the new class. Traditionally, they have sought power by indirect means—through persuasion and education. But this is unsatisfactory because it is slow and not necessarily successful. It is much better from their point of view to acquire power through legislation enabling them to tell people what to do and how to conduct their affairs. They see the free market economy as wasteful of resources.

Q: Fletcher Byrom, board chairman of Koppers Company, was quoted recently as saying "In five to 10 years we will be moving strongly in the direction of state control of capital-intensive industries. Our political system just won't allow corporations to make the profits they need." Does this seem probable to you?

KRISTOL: I think that is what is happening. The normal criterion of capital investment—return on capital—is being replaced to a degree by various political criteria to achieve various social or moral objectives. No one even thinks it particularly radical that members of Congress should be demanding that the Federal Reserve Bank siphon money into housing in preference to other activities. Yet it represents a startling departure from free market practice. It represents control over investment of capital. In the end, this is what will determine the shape of our society. If you have a free market system, then control over investment is determined by the market. The indicators are return on equity or investment. If you impose a system in which political criteria take precedence, then you don't pay much attention to the market.

Q: Why does a planned economy seem so appealing, then?

KRISTOL: Nothing is perfect, the market economy has its flaws. It tends to have cyclical ups and downs, for example—particularly in respect to employment. Members of the new class see in these flaws justification for trying something else. They will admit, for example, that the free market is the most productive of all systems. But they will say that with a little planning in the right places, it could be even more productive; and with a little regulation here and there the flaws could be eliminated. We'll keep only the good parts and get rid of the bad parts, they say. But that's unreasonable. If you want the benefits of a free market system then you must accept the costs as well, because a free market system cannot operate properly if it isn't free.

Q: Why does the new class disapprove of the free market system?

KRISTOL: From the viewpoint of the new class, the major cost of the free market comes from its effect on what they call the "quality of Life." They deplore the materialism which a free market system tends to produce. Ordinary people, who are not rich, have a lot of needs they want to satisfy. They express these needs in the marketplace. This means that the marketplace is primarily oriented toward satisfying the commonplace needs of ordinary people. This bothers the new class because it tends to produce a society that is not very elegant or brilliant. It is not a society that intellectuals and the educated classes are likely to admire. Intellectuals all over the world have serious reservations about our society. They don't like all those automobiles—all those brands of toothpaste—all those gas stations—all those ordinary people enjoying themselves in so many simple ways. They feel that society should not be shaped by the appetites of such people. The members of the new class feel that they, themselves, have something important to contribute to the quality of life. They feel that extraordinary people should have extraordinary influence over the shape of society, so as to create a life of suitable quality.

On the other hand, ordinary people the world over admire the United States. They all want to come here. They think it would be nice to have a society designed to satisfy their needs and cater to their preferences, even if the quality of such a life were regarded as less than admirable by some. I would say to the new class: it is true that the quality of life in the United States is not the highest. On the other hand, one of the great advantages of this kind of society is that it is a free society. That means that individuals or small groups are free to form their own world within this society and to achieve a quality of life within this society that suits them. That is really quite a lot. It suffices for me. But we will always have officious people who aren't satisfied with that and want to see the whole civilization change in ways which they quite sincerely think to be better.

Q: Are these people willing to sacrifice freedom to achieve these ends?

KRISTOL: Of course, they are. They tell themselves it won't be necessary. It would be impolitic to say, we want a less-free society. So, they say, we aren't going to sacrifice freedom. We're just going to use the political authority to intervene more directly in the life of the nation to give it a better shape for the benefit of all. But of course once the authority is used in that way, it's only a question of time before it will be abused. Where a latent threat to freedom exists, it will—sooner or later—become overt. We've seen it happen over and over again.

Q: Perhaps the growth of the new class would help explain the dwindling public confidence in our free market economy.

KRISTOL: Not entirely. As I said, Americans have always equated size with power, and looked upon bigness with suspicion and distrust. But it certainly seems reasonable that the new class, with its access to children in the classroom, and its access to adults through newspapers and television, would be inclined to reinforce the public's fears. This in turn would tend to ease the political problems involved in gaining legislative authority to control the economy. Certainly the new class, through the media, has helped to excite expectations among Americans that would be unreasonable in any society. It is in the nature of media to excite expectations. Everything has to be done immediately. All demands must be met now, regardless of cost. Our entire society seems to be encouraging this trend.

Q: Is such a trend normal to a democracy?

KRISTOL: I don't think so. I think it is what happens when a democracy goes soft and loses its moral fiber. We seem to have lost our capacity to be reasonable. When our demands aren't immediately gratified, we protest that our rights have somehow been violated. If this is the way American politics is going to go, with our politics focused on satisfying short-term demands, without respect to long-term consequences, then our political system is in severe trouble. It is a course that will take us more rapidly into state capitalism and a planned economy.

Q: Do you think those of us in the private sector should fight back?

KRISTOL: Absolutely. One of the reasons the new class has been so successful is that it has met so little opposition. Businessmen don't even seem to get indignant when some politician calls them nasty names. If you don't fight back, the American people won't respect you. It creates a healthier climate when businessmen defend themselves against erroneous accusations. It's very important that the media not get into the habit of being certain that politicians and bureaucrats are always right. Americans respect fighters who will defend their own interests. In American politics, it is perfectly legitimate for any group to defend its interests. Interest-group politics is American politics. There's nothing wrong with any interest group saying, we are against this because it hurts us.

Corporations are in trouble because they have no interest group to represent them, no constituency. Yet there are 33 million Americans who own shares in American business. They should become a constituency for the free market economy. When legislation or regulations are proposed that will have an adverse effect on a corporation, shareholders should step forward into the political process and say, Ouch! We're being hurt. We want you to know that we don't like it. That's American politics.

Q: What is at stake for Americans if we continue to move toward state capitalism and a planned economy?

KRISTOL: What is at stake is the question of individual liberty. You don't have to like corporations in order to think that their existence is important. Their existence in the private sphere is important to the existence of the private sphere in general. For the same reason, it is important for us to have private universities. Not that private schools are necessarily better than public schools. But they are private. They constitute a sector beyond the reach of government. That's the sector of freedom. To the degree that this sector shrinks, for any reason, to that degree individual liberty will also shrink. Therefore those of us who care about individual liberty also must care about institutions that exist in the private sector, even if we don't much like those institutions. Their existence is important for that sector and therefore important for what I regard as a satisfactory degree of individual freedom in this country.

CHAPTER 12

The Myth of American Imperialism[1]

The charge that the U.S.A. is guilty of "Imperialism" is repeated incessantly and believed without question by multitudes throughout the world as well as by many within this country.

Unfortunately the myth is usually unrefuted as many patriots and anticommunists do not understand what Imperialism means in its current usage.

This is tragic as verifiable facts make the change ridiculous.

There are two specific accusations in the doctrine of Imperialism. They can be summarized:

1. American prosperity, including the high wages of the workers, is due to the profits that result from the investment of U.S. capital in underdeveloped countries.
2. The investment of capital in underdeveloped countries is a technique to steal the natural resources of those countries and results in the impoverishment of the native people.

[1] Dr. Fred Schwarz, "The Myth of Imperialism," *Christian Anti-Communism Crusade*, June 1, 1976.

These charges are dramatized in this statement from the basic Weatherman document, "You don't need a Weatherman to show which way the wind blows." The Weathermen are currently urban guerrillas engaged in bombing and arson of U.S. banks and industrial enterprises. They were formerly outstanding students at such universities as Harvard, Columbia, Michigan, and California at Berkeley who were active in Students for a Democratic Society (SDS). The doctrine of Imperialism transformed them into violent enemies of their own country:

"We are within the heartland of a worldwide monster, a country so rich from its worldwide plunder that even the crumbs doled out to the enslaved masses within its borders provide for material existence very much above the conditions of the masses of people of the world. The US empire, as a worldwide system, channels wealth, based upon the labor and resources of the rest of the world, into the United States. The relative affluence existing in the United States is directly dependent upon the labor and natural resources of the Vietnamese, the Angolans, the Bolivians and the rest of the peoples of the Third World. All of the United Airlines Astrojets, all of the Holiday Inns, all of Hertz's automobiles, your television set, car and wardrobe already belong, to a large degree to the people of the rest of the world."

The charge that U.S. prosperity is due to the profits from overseas investment is completely refuted by the official statistics concerning overseas investments and the resultant profits. The following figures are taken from reports prepared by the Bureau of the Census and the Department of Commerce, as published in the American Almanac for 1976. The figures are for the year 1973 and are the latest available.

Table 1 shows that all the profits from U.S. overseas investments are less than one percent of wages paid to U.S. workers. If every cent of the profits were distributed to U.S. workers, it would account for less than one percent of the individual's wage.

Table I

Total U.S. Assets and Investments Abroad	$226,100,000,000
Total Assets and Investments of Foreigners in the U.S.A.	163,000,000,000
Net Foreign Investment of the U.S.A.	63,000,000,000
Total Income from U.S. Foreign Investments	13,984,000,000
Total Payment to Foreign Investors	8,694,000,000
Net Income from Foreign Investments	5,290,000,000
Total Wage Bill for U.S. Workers	786,000,000,000

Table II reveals that 71 percent of U.S. overseas investments is in Canada, Europe, Japan, Australia and New Zealand which are not underdeveloped countries.

Table II
Distribution of U.S. Foreign Investment

Canada	26%
Europe	34%
Japan	5%
Australia, New Zealand, and South Africa	6%
Latin America	14%
Africa (without South Africa)	3%
Middle East	3%
Asia (without Middle East and Japan)	4%
Others	5%

(The American Almanac, pages 799, 801, 802, 384)

The charge that U.S. investment in an underdeveloped country impoverishes that country is refuted by the present prosperity of the oil-producing Arab states. It was mostly U.S. capital that discovered the oil, drilled the wells, built the pipelines and refineries. The result is that these countries are today incredibly rich.

Overseas investment is like fire; it can be destructive or creative. It all depends upon how it is used.

It would be possible for an individual, who was against the use of fire, to compile a list of unspeakable human tragedies that have resulted from uncontrolled fire. This does not change the truth that controlled fire has proven to be man's greatest blessing. According to ancient mythology, it was the theft of fire from heaven that raised men to the rank of gods. It has certainly elevated man from savagery to civilization.

The doctrine of Imperialism is evil nonsense. It is itself the source of untold human suffering. Creative sharing of the accumulated fruits of human initiative and labor, through the controlled investment of capital in underdeveloped countries, is the path to deliverance from hunger, pestilence, and premature death.

CHAPTER 13

An Educator's Viewpoint: Bicentennial Message[1]

Why is the celebration of America's Bicentennial of such importance to the world, as well as to those of us who are blessed to be Americans?

The answer lies in the reasons for America's greatness. There is no denying the greatness of this nation. From an obscure beginning known as the American Revolutionary War, thirteen struggling Colonies won their freedom on the military field. That within itself is not unusual, but the leaders of those Colonies had won a more important battle long before the first shot of that war was fired. That battle was over the very nature of man, his origin, his purpose and his future. They fought with their muskets at Concord, Lexington, Valley Forge and Jamestown because they had achieved a high and noble concept of man. That is why their famous Declaration: "We hold these truths to be self-evident. That all men are created equal and are endowed by their Creator with certain unalienable rights such as life, liberty and the pursuit of happiness . . ."

They fought against the government of England and they

1 Dr. George S. Benson, "Bicentennial Message," *National Program*, May, 1976, pp. 3-4.

won their battle for freedom because they believed that ". . . to secure these rights, governments are instituted among men, deriving their just powers from the consent of the governed." As Thomas Jefferson put it elsewhere . . . "The freedom and happiness of man . . . these are the sole objects of legitimate government." So then July 4, 1976 is not just two hundred years of one form of government as opposed to another form. What we should be celebrating is the victory of a noble idea of man as opposed to the ignoble concept that government provides for the people instead of the people providing the government.

Let's spell it out so there can be no misunderstanding. The American Revolution was fought and won to establish the fact that MAN is a CREATED being, with the right of LIFE, LIBERTY and THE PURSUIT OF HAPPINESS. So, the American ship of state was launched on the sea of political existence based on an entirely new idea, that man should be free because God, his Creator, made him free in the act of creation. Man should be free because he is a created being, made in the image and likeness of his Creator. That no man has the right to take from another his liberty, and that no government has the authority to grant that which God has given in the act of Creation . . . inalienable rights.

Four decades ago, this nation was flooded with socialist ideas—the overall plan of utopia, the "planned economy." Federal agencies controlling the economic life of the nation became so numerous they were designed only by the use of the alphabet. In the midst of what came to be called "The Great Depression," there was launched in America a most determined effort to change the very basis of our system of government. Taking advantage of the dire circumstances of the depression, a group of "social planners" attached themselves to our national government in Washington and the war to destroy the "inalienable rights" of Americans began making progress for the first time.

The bureaucrats were empowered to take control over the products of farms. Farmers were paid for not growing crops. Pigs, cattle and sheep were slaughtered to satisfy the planners. All this during a time of "bread lines" and starvation. The slogan, "Tax, spend and elect" was the battle cry of the era to accomplish their socialistic programs.

The power to tax was the instrument to render dependent those who were not impoverished by the depression. The power to spend was the instrument to render dependent those who were impoverished. The power to tax and spend was a big help to re-elect those in charge of the government at the time. This is clear from the following statement from the book entitled, TAXATION FOR PROSPERITY, by Randolph E. Paul, Under Secretary of the Treasury at that time:

"Why do we have a Federal tax system? In answering this question we shall do well to break with tradition and think with open minds. The first item of business is to reject the gospel that taxes are for revenue only . . . We need to look at taxes in a more positive way as an instrument of social and economic control wholly apart, with revenue yield only part of the objective." Listen further to this socialistic philosphy . . . "The point is that taxes may be imposed, wholly apart from their revenue-producing qualities, to achieve desired effects on particular occasions . . . It is the highest function of taxes to accomplish positive social and/or economic objectives, beyond the revenue." Listen to still more of this socialistic thinking:

"On this higher level, taxes may be used to express public policy on the distribution of wealth and income: . . . They may be used to penalize particular industries and economic groups . . ." That is definitely socialism, not constitutional Americanism.

I affirm that the Constitution does not grant to Congress or to any bureau the right to penalize, by the taxing power, citizens who have not violated the law. Yet, the objective of the "social planners" both in and out of government at that time was made clear by Harold L. Ickes, Secretary of the Interior, by this entry in his diary: "We are working toward a society of modified Communism" (The Los Angeles Times, 7-16-35). Despite the efforts of a few to stop this movement calculated to change the very form of our government, with only a setback here or there to slow the progress, America has continued for the past forty years on a course directly opposite to its charter of 1776.

Another President, stated in 1964:

"We are going to take all the money we think is unnecessarily being spent, and take it from the 'haves' and give it the 'havenots.' (Cong. Rec. 1964, p. 2227, White House Speech of January 16, 1964). In short, Washington Bureaucrats with the power of Commissars, were to determine how much money of each citizen "is unnecessarily being spent."

Abraham Lincoln once said: "Any society that takes away from those most capable and gives to those least capable will perish." He also stated: "Our defense is in the spirit which prized liberty as the heritage of all men, in all lands everywhere. Destroy this spirit and you have planted the seeds of despotism at your doors." Today, from every dollar earned in America, an average of approximately 43.5 percent goes to pay taxes at all levels—federal, state and local. Should we balance our budget and continue current spending, the top rate would rise to 50% by 1978.

Summing up the broad principles included in A Message for the Bicentennial, Mr. A. Calder Mackay asks: "Will our Constitution, now hanging by a thread, survive the Bicentennial?" Cecil B. DeMille, in the language of an inspired patriot, gives the answer.

"The principle of the separation of church and state has never meant and need never mean the exclusion of moral and religious values from education or the exiling of God from our national life. If you believe that it does mean that, you must cut out of the Declaration of Independence its most potent clause . . . 'endowed by their Creator with certain inalienable rights' . . . and when you cut that out, you have cut out the heart that pumps the life blood of liberty through the nation's veins. If men will not be ruled by God, they will certainly be ruled by tyrants . . ."

". . . But if we believe, as did the founding Fathers, that the law of God is and must always be an American ideal, then it is worth the giving of the last ounce of our strength, the last drop of our blood, the last breath of our lives." (The Foundation of Freedom),—an address by Cecil B. DeMille at Baylor University, Oct. 12, 1957)."

Socialists are planning the funeral of man's liberty. What is your plan?

CHAPTER 14

If My People

The laws upon which individual freedom and independence were established represent the successful effort of our founding fathers to codify moral standards and fix penalties for those who will not observe these standards. They reached above the philosophers with their various intents and interpretations of life and derived their concepts of ethical ideals from the God of creation and Judge of nations. The fact that men have a spiritual dimension of supreme importance explains the dismal record of secular humanist philosophies throughout history. God exists! God being the Benefactor of our unalienable rights is the sanction for His claim to obedience and as Sovereign has promised to bless that nation which will pray and turn from its sins. "And can the liberties of a nation be thought secure when we have removed their only firm basis, a conviction in the minds of the people that these liberties are the gift of God?" (Thomas Jefferson, "Notes on the State of Virginia," 1782).

The substance of the law was the commandments. Instead of the anarchy of a society that has no laws and belief in God or the tyranny of a monarchy, we had an orderly civilization. Morality was not legislated. The guidelines were. Morality came with belief in God enlivened by education generally. Those who had the self-imposed manners to respect the life, liberty and possessions of others were at liberty in society. The antagonists to the Spirit of 1776 have constantly opposed the teaching of these ideals that stress independence because they do not help fit people for control by social programmers. The people with the strength of character upon which the greatness of America is dependent are inherently no better than their antagonists. They honestly face the reality of sin and judgment and the truth makes them free. Historically, those who violated the laws set to protect society were either caught and punished by the government or acted in secrecy to avoid punishment. Government power was so limited by restrictions on function and authority that it could not be used to degrade the spiritual or dictate and impede economic progress essential to freedom.

Our founding fathers had no faith in rule by the best of men and rightly so. A fundamental principle was fear of government over man. They found that "In God We Trust" works much better than any other basis for government that ever existed. There were many great problems but there was always progress.

When men cease to believe in God, their standards fade. Hence, no dependable standards can be translated into law. As we are finding, men who do not believe in God have few moral ideals upon which to erect a moral law. When faith in God disappears, moral standards disappear, individuals and families are torn apart and the civilization crumbles. Selfishness takes its toll in ignorance and distrust of the guidelines of a sovereign God, given to us to make true happiness possible.

The benefits of belief in God lead us to observe that freedom and economic well-being in society are possible only for men whose faith in God leads them to accept moral standards or commandments which cause them to tell the truth; this in turn gives the benefits of reliability in communications so important to representative government.

"Of all the dispositions and habits which lead to political prosperity, Religion and morality are indispensable supports. In vain would that man claim the tribute of

Patriotism, who should labour to subvert these great Pillars of human happiness, these firmest props of the duties of Men and citizens. The mere Politician, equally with the pious man ought to respect and to cherish them. A volume could not trace all their connections with private and public felicity. Let it simply be asked where is the security for property, for reputation, for life, if the sense of religious obligation *desert* the oaths, which are the instruments of investigation in Courts of Justice? And let us with caution indulge the supposition, that morality can be maintained without religion. Whatever may be conceded to the influence of refined education on minds of peculiar structure, reason and experience both forbid us to expect that National morality can prevail in exclusion of religious principle. 'Tis substantially true, that virtue or morality is a necessary spring of popular government." (Emphasis his)
(President George Washington, *Farewell Address*)

"Thou shalt not steal" promotes fairness and respect for the property of others so indispensable to liberty. "Thou shall not commit adultery" emphasizes the inviolability of the bond of family life, the foundation of all human society and order. "Thou shall not kill" gives sanctity to life and justice to harsh laws punishing its violators. If men believe the ideals come from God, they will observe them. If they have no God of truth and justice, men will seek acceptance, rationalization and philosophical niceness for acts of selfishness.

We are finding that when faith in God disappears, laws against crime are ignored or repealed. Elimination of teaching in public education of trust in the Creator and the absolutes of morality discredits in the minds of youth the very basis for obedience to laws and the liberating vitality of our Constitution. Long ago stricken from their vocabulary, sin can only be seen in the eyes of its victims who wonder, "Why?"

History's lesson is that when men arrive at this state the strong exploit the weak, and discipline is finally restored by the cruelty of a social dictator enslaving the people or by a spiritual revival unleashing a return to God's absolutes, a return of liberty and a return of political action by moral people.

In spite of the deteriorating situation in America, there is reason for hope. The evidence is that the bulk of the people, particularly in the tone-setting media such as education, who unwittingly participated in taking God out of our culture in the last sixty years have not been fairly and honestly dealt with. They have been imposed upon by parties and men assuming the characteristics of good leaders. It is time to honestly look at the leaders in the light of the principles of responsible freedom.

It is time also that the silent majority dismiss its inattentions to education and government, spend time voting, help good candidates and attend local precinct meetings. Every adult Christian in America who is not bedridden should attend his precinct meeting where the party planks and candidates get their grassroots start. Americans can be encouraged as they contemplate the promise of God to bless with good rulers when the people of the nation serve and obey Him. First Samuel 12:14 says, "If ye will fear the Lord, and serve him, and obey his voice, and not rebel against the commandment of the Lord, then shall both ye and also the king that reigneth over you continue following the Lord your God." In other words, included in serving God is the duty of His people to participate in the political process of selecting the President, the Representatives and the School Board. This may include the individual responsibility of free men setting up a good alternative to public education. Political and educational forces cannot be expected to give due emphasis to the God of creation unless Christians participate in politics. Inattention to these minimal duties has long been the encouraging cause in the deterioration of the forces of practical righteousness. It is time for us to dismiss our support of all those whose actions and platitudes are calculated to emancipate the mind from the wisdom of our founding fathers, as if this wisdom were too tentative to serve as an educational base. The disgusting picture of wretchedness so prevalent among people, skeptical of the wisdom embedded in the Spirit of 1776 should be reminder enough of the effect of lost principles. On this subject, men only have to open their eyes and think, and they will no longer be misled.

The people of other nations, including Israel, have forgotten God and His ethical teachings that civilize. And like the people of Israel all nations have this promise: "If my people, which are called by my name, shall humble themselves, and pray, and seek my face, and turn from their wicked ways; then will I hear from heaven, and will forgive their sin, and will heal their land" (II Chronicles 7:14).

One person can do a lot. Many significant elections are decided by less than one vote per precinct. The election of Lyndon B. Johnson to the Senate in 1948 and the election of John Kennedy in 1960 over Richard Nixon for President are examples. It is not unusual for School Board members to be elected by less than five percent of the electorate. Frequently less than one-tenth of one percent of the people in a precinct attend the local precinct meetings of either major political party. In such a case, the voice of one Christian could be that of hundreds of people that are absent. A duty is a duty; civic rent, if you please, for our liberty. Having participated in politics, one can die with a clear conscience, knowing he has lived a life worthy of our great heritage. One million Christians could turn the tide and extend freedom for the glory of God! It should start with you and me and continue as long as we have breath!

CHAPTER 15

Government

The definition of liberty we have dealt with focuses on the shepherd, the individual independent and free, not on the wolf, or collectivist overlords of government. The shepherd's responsibility to his Creator and to his family along with the right to prosperity through the fruits of his labor frees him from the interdependence or servitude that comes when beholden to government planners.

How is censorship in education by tyrants of the mind affecting man's discernment and ability to steer government aright? Asking the question, we ponder the indicators of progress and see that in the humanities we are much worse off than we were seventy years ago. Today our rockets soar into space to inspect new horizons of God's creation because in the physical sciences of engineering and chemistry the education of new scientists is based upon absolutes and established knowledge. The humanists train their new scientists to seek truth by denying the absolutes and established knowledge.[1]

1 "We know that we have made no discoveries; and we think that no discoveries are to be made in morality; nor many in the great principles of government, nor in the idea of liberty, which were understood long before we were born, altogether as well as they will be

98

Prayer and the affirmative teaching of trust in God are cen-
sored from classroom and textbooks. Homosexuals, communists and secular humanists get the podium in some public
schools.

What has displacing fundamental faith in the non-sectarial
God of our Republic and His law with secular humanism in
our schools done to self-discipline, ethics, and morality? And
what has this done to the vitality of our Constitution?

FEAR OF GOVERNMENT OVER MEN

Probably, second in importance only to the spiritual nature
of man and recognizing God as the source of our rights is the
traditional American philosophy—fear of government over
man. Mere lip service to the phrase limited government is of
no value to freedom. The treacherous nature of government
that requires constant concern stems from the fact that government servants are fallible and the power granted in operating government is very harmful when misused and much
more devastating than the mistakes of individuals dispersed
throughout society. Some large projects are in the public interest and should be handled by government. Size of government or even the deplorable graft of public officials is not the
imminent danger to our freedom, however.

The double jeopardy of government is unleashed when collectivists are given the reigns over inputs that can destroy
freedom's cultural tone!! Delegation of power in these areas
has the effect of not only giving the employee men and
women of government the added temptation, but also giving
the power to use his position and the public treasury to raise
himself up as master over the people.

Government is like a fire—a dangerous servant and a fear-
ful master. To be useful, it must be strictly controlled for the
safety from its getting out of hand. The following are illustrative of our founding fathers' debate on this principle.

---

after the grave has heaped its mould upon our presumption, and the
silent tomb shall have imposed its law on our pert loquacity." Edmund
Burke

" . . . In questions of power then let no more be heard of confidence in man, but bind him down from mischief by the chains of the Constitution."

Thomas Jefferson
(Kentucky Resolutions, 1798)

"Ever present weaknesses of human nature in government which are conducive to love of power and proneness to abuse it."

(Washington's Farewell Address)

" . . . experience hath shewn, that even under the best forms (of government), those entrusted with power have, in time, and by slow operations, perverted it into tyranny . . ."

Thomas Jefferson
("Diffusion of Knowledge" Bill in
Virginia Legislature, 1779)

"Show me that age and country where the rights and liberties of the people were placed on the sole chance of their rulers being good men, without a consequent loss of liberty! I say that the loss of that dearest privilege has ever followed, with absolute certainty, every such mad attempt."

Patrick Henry
(Virginia Ratifying Convention, 1788)

The greater portion of our Constitutional Law was penned to protect the people from abuse of government. Government abuse has come as the collectivist battering ram has shattered belief in the traditional American philosophy and censorship in education, has blunted our sensitivity to abuses in the Constitutional guidelines and the important reasons for restricted government power.

GOVERNMENT SHOULD NOT

The greatest cause of harmful governmental trends today is, of course, the impact of tyrants of the mind upon the cap tive audience of public schools. The fallacy of entrusting the control of history, government and social studies curriculum to collectivist educators or planners is obvious. Faith in God, the family and the Spirit of 1776 have suffered terribly from the deceptive and slanted presentation of collectivist educators.

Their blatant attack upon the basic belief in the God of Creation is illustrated by their success in the politicizing of science curriculum and saddling science with Darwinian theories. Their denial of God as the Creator of life is as scientific as the theory taught in ancient times that the world is square. This is devastating to freedom when forced upon the captive audience of youth.

For some students who find themselves in this situation, school must seem like a prison without God, where they are tormented and confused spiritually, not knowing who to trust or where to turn.

Without being told the truth about the Spirit of 1776 in an affirmative way, how can mankind learn, except through the fire of experience? How can the voters distinguish between the unglamorous proposals for sound government and glamorous promises of politicians who would buy votes either knowingly or unknowingly at the cost of liberty?

GOVERNMENT SHOULD NOT

Another cause of social corruption is bureaucrats taking over the common citizen's right and responsibility to be the jury over who among our citizens is honestly and unavoidably in need of funds from the public treasury for daily living. The destructive effect of abuses here upon the character of people and the polarization of the irresponsible voters to collectivist political advantage is apparent today.

GOVERNMENT SHOULD NOT

Another aspect of government that is so framed with the

fire of social injustice and tyranny over the people is side stepping justice in our penal system. Collectivists have had limited results in tampering with the citizen juries. What they are doing in their elitist secular wisdom is to abuse justice by turning the criminal loose on society even when our citizen jury finds the defendant guilty. We are now seeing the great harm that is done to society and our cultural tone when government officials give favors by turning the criminals loose.

The collectivists have an endless list of excuses that local citizen control cannot be handled administratively. They make liberal use of the words such as economy, justice and human dignity to argue and batter down citizen control.

Before our Constitution can again become effective, we must absolutely abandon confidence in any man and government and again assert our proper citizen role over these delicate factors that can destroy freedom's cultural tone.

As wrong as these injustices are from the hand of government collectivists, this is the inevitable consequence and practice that follows as numbers of our society have the collectivist mentality saddled upon them by tyrants of the mind.

Not only is the common man the only safe reservoir for the power to make the decisions that affect the cultural tone of the people, but the experience and exercise of these duties are also essential for the people. The success of collectivists in securing these duties from the people aggravates and promotes the weakening of the self-governed people themselves.

We are now seeing a rekindling of state sedition laws so helpful during the first century in America.[2] They will not be effective however unless supported by alert citizens politically. Freedom will survive if the people know the truth through "diffusion of knowledge" rather than censoring absolutes. They will then understand and can clean up at the local level,

[2] Joint Interim Study Committee, Indiana State Legislature, chaired by Senator Gene E. Snowden, adopted on October 5, 1976, a bill designed to outlaw "regionalism" in the State, provide criminal sanctions for violators and authorize civil action for parties injured by "regionalism." Titled, A BILL FOR AN ACT TO AMEND THE SEDITION ACT OF 1919. "Offenses Against the Stability of the State," the bill was submitted to the Indiana Legislative Council, Oct. 20, 1976. (Committee to Restore the Constitution, Inc., Nov. 1976 Bulletin. Fort Collins, Colorado 80521).

the state level and finally resist the bold grabs for power over the people by collectivists in Federal Government.

The great distance that we have slipped educationally is apparent from this testimony by Thomas Jefferson on the open "eyes" and "spread of light" some 150 years ago.

"All eyes are opened, or opening to the rights of man. The general spread of the light of science has already laid open to every view the palpable truth that the mass of mankind has not been born with saddles on their backs, nor a favored few booted and spurred, ready to ride them legitimately by the grace of God."[3]

It is grossly inconsistent and unfair to the cause of freedom for government planners and others to attack the common man because he is not an expert in everything. The ultimate end to this attack cannot begin to justify the temporary benefit of another government program.

American greatness is the proof that man over limited government has no equal. Although collectivist leaders usually prosper personally, what happens to the socialized nation and to people is also proof that the specific and unique principles of American government have no equal.

These principles of limited government and citizen responsibility brought much of the world out of the dismal consequence of secular rationalist philosophy. Social and economic justice and keeping citizens instead of government, vested through ownership and alert through education and experience was largely ignored until the founding of America.

In the eyes of a collectivist, limited government is clumsy and ungainly. The common man keeps strings tied to the government that is his servant. To the collectivist it would be ridiculous to call a potluck for parents at the local school to be followed by a meeting to decide the fate of a school teacher who ignores teaching standards based on the unique and specific principles of American government. In fact, this would be a violation of the self-proclaimed right and prerogative of collectivist dictators. To leave the power in the hands of the common people as God-given, would destroy their se-

[3] Thomas Jefferson, leading spokesman for the Spirit of 1776 in his letter to R. C. Wightman, June 24, 1826.

curity needed to use public education as a haven to propagate socialist thought. To the collectivist planner, it may be dangerous and foolish, but it works much better than yielding such decisions to elitist dictation, local or regional.

This is not only true of the decisions over social studies curriculum in education and welfare programs that can be so destructive to the cultural tone of the people, it is also true of the market place.

FREE ENTERPRISE VERSUS SOCIALISM

In the free enterprise system protected by law from government or other monopolies, each producer is well-regulated because he is competing against others for consumer acceptance of his product. The citizens work, save and buy property. This property is their vested interest in freedom and motivation to work and be responsible citizens. The economic resources needed for daily living are kept in the hands of the common man where they are safe from the tyranny of bureaucrats. When elitists get the people to delegate their power over the root elements of society, the results are plain to see the world over; from Hitler's socialist Germany to the Soviet Socialist Republics down to the milder forms of socialism.

The quality of life under collectivist control deteriorates as the people lose the experience of self-government and the incentive to work. Public interest reflected in citizen safety, health, ecology, etc., suffers significantly under socialist collectivist regimes. Compare, for instance, the ecology and care of residential properties owned by the State and properties owned by the citizens themselves. Similar analogies can be made between the quality of service that medical doctors render as State agents, and the service rendered when they are paid by the citizens who have the money and freedom to choose their doctor. Once collectivist bureaucrats are in control, they can, of course, shift the monies they tax and provide super services to this group or that. They can do what they want until the nation's wealth is dissipated, then public interest becomes victim of not only unrealistic goal levels but bureaucrat distribution or manipulation. Socialist trends in America have caused many citizens to interpret the temporary relief from responsibility as political greatness. This sense of security is lethal.

The tyrants of the mind are loathe to explain justice as it relates to the inhuman conditions of poverty throughout much of the world. They are loathe to explain the blessing that came in America from the hands of common men and women capitalists operating independently of elitist bureaucrats or anyone else except the God of creation. It is easy to see why collectivists want to destroy the proper respect for the profit motive and ownership by the common people within society.

The book, *Tragedy and Hope* written by Dr. Carroll Quibley, a very learned and capable writer, explained that among the very first Americans to join the secret British Round Table, which was dedicated to creating a socialist world, was the leadership of our most distinguished universities. Is it any wonder that the Gallup Poll taken in 1975 found that the average high school student in America believed that corporate profits averaged about 35 per cent? College students believed that corporate profits were about 45 per cent. This demonstrates one of the reasons why so many high school and college students believe that private enterprise is not in the best interest of the nation. They are reflecting the attitudes of teachers and general critics but are quite ignorant of the facts. For instance, during no year in the last thirty have corporate profits averaged more than 6 per cent. Private enterprise, in addition to allowing liberty, pays far higher wages than do the industries of a socialist or communist country.

A modern day parallel to collectivist politicalization in America is the sobering story of the social labor government of Australia.[4] The Australian voters turned the collectivists out on December 9, 1975. Their new Prime Minister, Malcolm Fraser, referring to the social-economic havoc and attitude fostered under the socialists:

4 Australia's government deficit amounted to 5 per cent of its Gross National Product. In 1976, the U.S. deficit rose about 4 per cent of it's Gross National Product.

". . . the view had begun to develop that we could have it all without really having to pay for it. But one of the things we've got to understand is that when politicians promise things, they are not promising anything of their own, because they have nothing of their own to give. They are promising something which is *yours*, and the more politicians promise, the less there is for you to meet your own needs or your family's needs. The less there is for industry, for investment, and to create jobs needed to improve the real wealth of Australia."[5]

The more decisions that come under the power of government bureaucracy, the less debate there is! The opportunity for the common man to participate, to see results from personal expressions of what he knows, and to grow as a responsible citizen diminishes. As we are now seeing in our communities, the motivation for political activity is shifting to those who want to dictate the affairs of others and those so concerned they openly oppose the collectivist predators get cast as "specious and self-serving and unworthy of intelligent people."

Where are the leaders that America was known for in the first century? Where are the statesmen and cultural leaders who supported the idea that the common man is indeed capable, when under God, of knowing actions that affect others also affect himself? They are here nestled and crushed in the vast wasteland of education and cultural oblivion that has deprived them of the right to the truth about history and American principles of government.

But what is government to do? Our political leaders have been meddling in the precious balance of creative human enterprise and wisdom gained down through the ages and individual development, but what should it be doing? Men are endowed by their Creator with certain unalienable rights that among these are Life, Liberty and the Pursuit of Happiness, "that to *secure* these rights *governments are instituted* among men."

5 Anthony Paul, "The Sobering Story of Australia's Big Spending," *Reader's Digest*, January 1977.

WHAT SHOULD GOVERNMENT DO?

How has education's failure to support the principles of 1776 affected the government's fulfilling its function of keeping *secure* our right to life and liberty?

What is government doing to fulfill its duty to protect America from criminals from abroad?

The Independent National Education Program's periodical dated December, 1976 entitled "John Rarick" says, "KGB Espionage agents infiltrate congressional offices." The periodical reports on the findings of the Rockefeller Commission while investigating the CIA.

Ultra-professional Soviet KGB espionage agents have concentrated their spy activities on Capitol Hill, where congressional offices leak classified information like rusty buckets.

As explosive as this blatant KGB spying in the halls of Congress is, it is not the full story. High ranking government officials and U.S. intelligence agencies know of the foreign infiltration and are attempting to cover the spy network.

The Rockefeller Commission reportedly heard testimony behind closed doors earlier in the spring of 1976 which exposed an intricate KGB espionage network operating on Capitol Hill and revealed the ability of the Soviets to intercept congressional and White House telephone calls.

A massive KGB eavesdropping operation conducted from the Soviet Embassy was able to monitor as many as 100,000 long distance phone calls to and from the Hill.

The Soviet net has intercepted calls from every member of Congress at one time or another, which raises the possibilities of espionage blackmail by the Russians.

The June 23, 1976, *Des Moines Register* reported Soviet penetration of White House and Capitol Hill telephone conversations by one informed source as "hundreds of thousands, even millions."

Soviet-block agents operating under "deep cover" have been placed in congressmen's offices and on key committees, the commission learned. Operating as "agents of influence" the undisclosed number of Capitol Hill aides—whose salaries are paid by the U.S. taxpayers—have been able to loot secret and highly sensitive documents from the offices in which they work. The information has been turned over to professional KGB contacts who roam throughout the Capitol complex, immune from FBI surveillance.

A six-page draft section on the extent of Soviet KGB penetration into congressional offices was prepared by the Commission for its report. But that section was never released.

Some of the staffers are left-wing sympathizers, while others are co-opted into working with the Communists.

This "liberty" given our enemies for some twenty-five years now, combined with improper liberties of more and more of our senators, congressmen, judges and administrators illustrates the decay that precedes cultural starvation and educational abdication of the specific and uniquely American principles of individual responsibility to the Creator and to our nation.

This liberty is the excellence that the secular humanist philosophy has to offer. This is the record of people who are bigger than their founding fathers and bigger than God. Education with the principles based upon belief in God and the Judeo-Christian teaching of right and wrong is not good enough for them. They must in their great statesmen manner provide a self-made rationalization of right and wrong to ease their consciences. The standards of the world provide the norms for their life. Pride has even eaten up their common sense.

" . . . it is Pride which has been the chief cause of misery in every nation and every family since the world began. Other vices may sometimes bring people together: you may find good fellowship and jokes and friendliness among drunken people or unchaste people. But Pride always means enmity—it is enmity. And not only enmity between man and man, but enmity to God ....Pride........is the complete anti-God state of mind."[6]

Sin has ceased to exist, a pillar in the spectrum of knowledge, it is the victim of censorship.

[6] From *Mere Christianity* by C. S. Lewis.

TIME FOR SELF-ANALYSIS—BOTH LIBERALS AND CONSERVATIVES

Why the nausea among teachers and textbook writers over the concept of God our Creator and Judge as affirmatively taught in support of our government in public schools for most of our history? Why the malicious abuse of academic responsibility and twisting the meaning of academic freedom? Freedom has definite limits! Liberty is not a license to criminal purveyance over demonstrable truth! Education that does not indoctrinate and inculcate students with the principles of 1776 without weaseling one way or the other should not get one penny from American taxpayers.

This gives evil activity legitimacy. It should not have legitimacy! As long as it continues we are inviting collectivists to invade our institutions and destroy our nation. It must be corrected through a diffusion of knowledge! Schools that condone such perversion should be abandoned in favor of good sound schools that are on the side of human responsibility and liberty.

What a disgraceful situation for a nation that at one time was respected by all and feared by her enemies. Is it any wonder that the communists and their sympathizers in the press and our universities know in advance and counter with lies and half-truths nearly every strong move by our Presidents to get peace and victory over communist aggression as it enslaves one victim after another around the world?

The secular humanist do-gooder derides World Wars I and II stressing the inhumanity. At least we faced the inevitable inhumanity of an enemy conquest unstopped; at least the collectivist planners of Italy, Germany and Japan were crushed and beaten into submission and their enslaved people liberated from the inhumanity of the dictators. At least the American men and women who sacrificed many years of life through death on the battlefield did not die in vain! What is the secular humanist activist passion for humanity accomplishing for the liberation of those under communism and other totalitarians today?

Although there are many teachers who see the folly and ignore the professionals who censor God and moral absolutes from curriculum, is it any wonder that many of our new generation senators, congressmen, judges, councilmen, and teachers do not even understand and believe in the principles of our founding?

What other conclusion can the people whose minds are void of any understanding of the meaning of "In God we trust" come to?

Is it any wonder that support for socialist legislation and collectivist programs is pushing out from so many of our high schools and university campuses? Is it any wonder that collectivist politicians are being propelled to top positions in government? Is it any wonder that many councilmen and others in government fall for utopian ideas of health, safety, equality, ecology, and welfare and see it in terms as their divine rights as kings to take away through regulation and taxation the independence of the common men and women? They are predators in deed, destroying the citizens who are the very avenue of hope for progress; all because those who would govern were not taught the unique and specific American principles of government. Is it any wonder many abuse their families, live playboy lives and defiantly argue it is not of concern to the voters? They see no violation against society in their actions and ignore the foundations of morality upon which both national and individual continuance and prosperity is dependent. Is it any wonder our taxes increase and increase as they treat symptoms but ignore the basic cause of our problems?

Though all men in all ages for all time had ignored their responsibility to their Maker and Benefactor, though the most sophisticated schemes of the most lucid minds would try, the anvil will not bend.

"Genuine human freedom is given to us by God. Freedom to decide upon our own acts as well as the moral responsibility for theirs."[7]

---

[7] Russian author Alexander Solzhenitsyn remarks upon receiving the American Freedom Medal of Freedoms Foundation, Valley Forge at special ceremonies at Hoover Institution, Palo Alto, CA, June 1, 1976.

CHAPTER 16

Conclusion: Urgent Call to Action

The overriding problem in America today is that the humanities courses and teacher training in many of our tax supported schools have been taken over by men and women of the same stripe that at other times politicized the church or military, and in coalition with government held the masses in subjection through censorship of information. How long will freedom survive? Can it again thrive? Nearly all claim they are working toward these things that make a better America.

The lesson interwoven in any analysis of freedom and from which all our diverse but apparent problems stem is "Except the Lord build the house they labor in vain that build it . . ." (Psalm 127:1). One of our founding fathers spoke these words when haggling seemed to threaten establishment of our limited government, and he besought the men that they should pray and re-orient their motives and honesty to God's standards.

Never since the founding of our nation have circumstances so demanded that American citizens understand the basis and the dangers to the cultural tone that gave us freedom. At home and abroad tyrants of the mind and bureaucratic collectivists threaten with their "liberation." The very foundations

111

of a rule of law are bending to their counter-revolution that sees no obligation to build a solid foundation for society.

Since 1973 the portion of the world's population that remains free has gone from approximately 32% to 19.6%. Alexander Solzhenitsyn, Daniel Patrick Moynihan and others are trying to alert us. Stability of leadership and nations are split assunder as they abandon moral absolutes and the right of private ownership by the common man. Sin ceases to be acknowledged as man's enemy.

Newly realized energy shortages give some undeveloped nations, whose basic political foundations are still being determined, greater power than they ever dreamed of having. New accommodations among nations signal a whole new situation for international relations while strangulations of individual initiative and self-reliance go on here in America.

Such factors make the setting upon which we must evaluate and think through the meaning of freedom and human dignity and how best to strengthen them. To this end it is vital to communicate to American students an understanding of the source of our freedom and the cultural tone which sustains it.

It is important that we understand the nature of basic world conflict, for it is a struggle between two ways of life, between two approaches toward the human being and his destiny. It is a struggle between the forces of freedom and those who want to force a controlled society upon mankind.

Any successful approach naturally involves going back to fundamentals. "Before You Lose It All!" is meant to be a handbook or text on the mood of liberty. There has to be a right spirit, a personal attitude, a personal commitment to God, to family and to country. Attention is directed towards an understanding of the basic underpinnings of a free society such as we have developed in America and an understanding of the fundamentals of totalitarian systems and the operational code by which their proponents deceive and elbow into the cultural tone to undermine the fundamentals of freedom.

The Judeo-Christian teachings, upon which our government is based, provide the impregnable foundation for the sound ethics of rational self-interest for each person in society. Each person contributes to a strong, constructive and enduring community where men can move in a complex world with the God of creation as the common denominator. This nullifies the hold of collectivist and elitist predators and contributes to a reasonably high plane, morally and governmentally, in a manner consistent with the duty factor of individual liberty. It is true that even with education and other cultural media affirmatively promoting the Creator concept as a basis so essential to our Constitution there will still be some violators of the standard, but they constitute exceptions which demonstrate and help prove the value of the Judeo-Christian teaching. The benefit from this code of life transcends the changes in transportation, industry and science.

Taxing, consolidating and spending in public schools, even quadrupled will not produce the caliber of leaders that the impoverished, almost non-existent, schools of early America did. "In God We Trust" as an educational base, has no peer or substitute.

Just as fire destroys the ecology, the beauty of a virgin forest, bureaucratic paternalism destroys man. *Artificial and feigned relief from personal responsibility by government quenches the greatness of men and begets national decay.*

The collectivists want socialism and say that limited government as developed in America is inhumane; yet the very marrow of the bones of countless millions enslaved past and present cry in unison—"Socialism does not work."

The wolves or collectivist predators of government disagree with our definition of liberty. They are offended when they are prevented from manipulating the shepherd and the sheep.

One of the greatest proofs of God's power to turn things around today is to contemplate the enormous problems of early Americans. That small band of humble pilgrims on the Mayflower, who covenanted to glorify God, and their successors, the leaders of 1776, brought to the world within a few generations the mightiest nation of all nations. Americans read their *McGuffey Readers*. There was no mass manipulation; Americans were responsible individuals under God.

Let's do our duty!! This will mean withdrawing public funding from tyrants of the mind or, if this proves impossible, using our freedom while we still have it to place our children in good private schools at great personal financial sacrifice. It may mean being a candidate for the school board or other sensitive jobs that help determine the fate of freedom. It may mean refunding a government subsidy after seeing the present danger legislative handouts are to our nation. It will definitely mean taking time to vote and attending precinct meetings of your political party. Precinct meetings ought to be a fun time for Christians—they should be able to see all their friends there! It means withdrawing support of secular humanist-orientated institutions, and lending support to the many good organizations and churches which alert and inform our citizens. It will mean obedience to God, our just and worthy calling that leaves no room for codling tyrants of the mind.

Indoctrination of students in the specific and traditional principles of American government does not hinder the freedom and prosperity of the common people. The people that these principles hinder are the collectivists—the tyrants of the mind, the secular humanists. They oppose belief in God because such belief makes men and women unfit for collectivist manipulation. Their attack upon freedom's cultural tone is so unfair that the disgraced Senator McCarthy tactics, when compared, look good. Senator McCarthy's tactics were not good! Collectivists' misuse of freedom for maliciousness is similar to the tactics of the young corporate executive who stole the key to the company's computer information bank. By censoring out basic information going to other executives in the company he caused them to blunder in their decisions. Through this method he passed up nearly all the other members of the company. Some of the older executives had strong roots and were not misled. He proceeded to get them in submission or get rid of them and replace them with his henchmen. He did this by watching them closely and whenever they made a mistake, as we all do, he would attack them fiercely and repeatedly with verbal abuses and public criticism. If there was no resistance he would just continue the attack and do as much damage as he could. If they resisted he might back off a little then attack or he could back off completely; the option was his.

Like tyrants of the mind teaching the captive audience in public schools, he did not earn his position by the honest competition of ideas and work but by deception, censorship and malicious utterances.

As it was in this instance and as it is when secular rational philosophies get the upper hand, he ruined the institution. By the time he got caught, the place was a shambles. After surveying the damage the leaders decided it would be easier to start up a new company than it would be to clean out and restore the existing one.

The young corporate executive and his henchmen were nothing better than decadent scoundrels. Similarly the secular rational collectivists, the tyrants of the mind, are raping our institutions, our boys and girls and freedom. Their attack is not the onslaught of guns and tanks and ships, it is the plundering of the spirit and the mind and the soul. It is here that we must counterattack. It is here that we must humbly but forcefully assert our ideals and succeed and war for liberty.

Each new generation of Americans has a right, a God-given right, to the truth. Public servants hired to staff class-rooms have an unalterable duty to God, to the public, to the students, and to the state and nation under whose Constitution they live to affirmatively teach the specific and traditional American principles of government.

AMERICAN PRINCIPLES

The following are among the specific and unique American principles of government.

These principles, some of which we have documented and explored, are essential roots to freedom's cultural tone. The citizens must know and cling to this heritage or there is no hope for freedom!

I. The spiritual nature of each individual is held as being supremely important.

". . . all men are created . . . endowed by their Creator. . ."

(Declaration of Independence 1776)

This fundamental principle underlying the traditional American philosophy delineates man's relationship with God. This belief has a most beneficial effect upon the reasoning on all other matters. Men are not things that evolved, as modern secular elite theorize. Individuals have a spiritual and religious nature. Belief in the Divine origin of men and women is the foundational principle that gives the essential perspectives in establishing government.

There is a moral code that insures success. The individual's duty requires obedience to God's Law. Justice, self-respect, mutual respect and liberty from government tyranny go hand in hand.

II. God and God alone is the source of our unalienable rights.

"The God who gave us life gave us liberty at the same time; the hand of force may destroy, but cannot disjoin them."

Thomas Jefferson
("Rights of British America" 1776)

" . . . endowed by their Creator with certain unalienable Rights . . ."

(Declaration of Independence)

Because of the origin of our rights, collectivist government officials who violate this truth, presuming to be the dispensers of rights, do a great injustice to man and the truth. Such abuse interferes with man's sacred right and God-given capacity to be self-governing and personally secure for the purpose of life and the pursuit of happiness.

III. All men are equal in God's sight and before the law.

" . . . all men are created equal . . ."

(Declaration of Independence)

This traditional premise in American philosophy emphasizes the God-given equality men have in a religious spiritual sense and the legal sense.

Individuals quite obviously are not equal to others in size or talent. Justice does require, by God's standards, that each individual be recognized as being equal spiritually and therefore entitled to equal legal justice before the law. This entitles each to freedom from the injustice of moral polluters of secular, rational philosophy. Government is to be limited to "just powers" designed to provide security for their equal rights as individuals. These rights are a part of and consistent with the natural law (God-given duties and benefits).

This is basic to the right of men and women to be protected by the law; having their freedom equally protected from all freedom predators, chief of which is government itself.

IV. Life and the pursuit of happiness—humanity's goal.

" . . . unalienable rights, that among these are life . . . and the pursuit of happiness."

(Declaration of Independence)

This aspect of our American philosophy focuses quite remarkably upon something that is rather hard to define—the goal of mankind throughout history. All generally want happiness, the big problem has been that some, rather than working and earning their own, wish to get it by taking from others.

The direction one goes in the pursuit of happiness is up to the individual as long as it does not interfere with the liberty of others. Our traditional principles of government are to protect the individual from liberty's offenders, but does not presume the vain hope that it can provide happiness. Happiness comes when men are at peace with their Creator, their fellow men and their environment. It is a challenge to each and every individual for which no one else can answer.

V. Liberty—a gift of God, desirable and beneficial.

" . . . unalienable rights, that among these are . . . liberty . . ."

(Declaration of Independence)

Although it has been their lot generally throughout history, people are not things for hiding in obscurity or mass manipulation. Criminal elements or others who do not know better may spook them in one direction or another with propaganda. People may blunder and become slaves because of the injustice of censorship or politicized information.

People by nature want freedom. They may be imprisoned and very well fed, kept in warm and comfortable surroundings, but they still are not happy. In the sight of God and those who trust in God, people not only desire freedom, they are capable of and created for freedom; each person has a soul that lives forever and is far more important than the temporal state or material things. Individuals are endowed by God with the will power and the intellect to be accountable and this makes liberty possible. When, and only when, man's spiritual nature is respected and the people are told the truth about God and nature, do they successfully pursue happiness and experience liberty.

Liberty includes freedom from any that trap, manipulate, pollute and spoil, not the least of which is government over man.

VI. Private ownership of property—indispensable to liberty.

(Recommending that each Colony form a new government) " . . . and it is necessary that . . . all the powers of Government (should be) exerted, under the authority of the people of the colonies, for the preservation of internal peace, virtue, and good order, as well as for the defence of their lives, liberties and properties . . ."

(Resolutions, Continental Congress,
May 15, 1776)

" . . . the great end of government . . . (after the glory of God, is) . . . the good of man, the common benefit of society . . . instituted for the preservation of mens persons, properties and various rights . . ." (Per the original).

Rev. Jonathan Mayhew
(Election Sermon, 1754)

"That Government is instituted and ought to be exercised for the benefit of the people; which consists in the enjoyment of life and liberty, with the right of acquiring and using property, and generally of pursuing and obtaining happiness and safety."

James Madison
(In 1st Session of Congress of U.S.,
in proposing "Bill of Rights" amendments to U.S. Constitution)

" . . . The Utopian schemes of levelling, and a community of goods, are as visionary and impracticable, as those which vest all property in the Crown, are arbitrary, despotic, and in our government unconstitutional."

House of Representatives of Massachusetts
(1768, to agent in London for the Colonies)
(Note: the word "unconstitutional" pertains to the British "Constitution")

" . . . our wish . . . is, that . . . (there be maintained) . . . that state of property, equal or unequal, which results to every man from his own industry, or that of his fathers."

President Thomas Jefferson
(Second Inaugural Address)

"Property must be secured, or liberty cannot exist."

John Adams
("Discourses on Davila," 1790)

"There is not a single instance in history in which civil liberty was lost, and religious liberty preserved entire. If therefore we yield up our temporal property, we at the same time deliver the conscience into bondage."

Rev. John Witherspoon
(Sermon, May 17, 1776)

"Agriculture, manufactures, commerce, and navigation, the four pillars of our prosperity, are the most thriving when left most free to individual enterprise."

President Thomas Jefferson
(Message to Congress, 1801)

The right of the common men and women to own property liberates them from the necessity of bowing to the state for material gratuities. Property ownership is the common person's vested interest in liberty. It provides great motivation for the citizen to work hard to be productive and thrifty. To respect labor, to respect property and to take good care of things.

VII. Government is to be feared.

Because of the failure to contain government and the subtleness in which its officials tend to violate safe limits, it has led generally to the enslavement and impoverishment of mankind. This, among the most emphatic lessons that history has to offer, was, fortunately for us, correctly interpreted by our founding fathers (see chapter 15).

VIII. Government must be limited in function.

Governments are limited and derive "their just powers from the consent of the governed."
(Declaration of Independence)

The history of individual liberty is the history of the effective limitation of government power. The nonsense of secular humanist liberalized justice has no place in government planning if it is to be kept at safe limits (see chapter 15).

IX. Government is therefore organized to be a tool and a tool only.

"That to secure these (God-given) rights, Governments are instituted among Men . . ."
(Declaration of Independence)

This principle of 1776 was revolutionary and is now being contested very aggressively by secular collectivists. Government is not the benefactor; it is only a tool. It can only disperse what it first takes away from the people. Thus, the people have the right and duty to be and stay sovereign. The people keep government as a servant by personally being the jury over policy matters that affect society's cultural tone. Government officials are public servants and wholly subservient to the people; their masters and superiors. When this principle is adhered to, not only in theory but also in practice, the individual has liberty from the injustice of bureaucrat commands and decrees. (see chapter 15).

X. Government decentralized—powers diffused.

" . . . true barriers (bulwarks) of our liberty are our State governments."
Thomas Jefferson

"A well regulated Militia, being necessary to the security

of a free State, the right of the people to keep and bear
Arms, shall not be infringed."

(U.S. Constitution, 2nd Amendment)

(As to danger of the Supreme Court's misinterpreting
the Constitution so as to concentrate power in Washington). "To this I am opposed; because, when all government . . . shall be drawn to Washington . . . it will
render powerless the checks . . . will become as venal
and oppressive . . . (as Great Britain's government)
. . . If the States look with apathy on this silent descent
of their government into the gulf which is to swallow all,
we have only to weep over the human character formed
uncontrollable but by a rod of iron, and the blasphemers
of man, as incapable of self-government, become his true
historians."

Thomas Jefferson
(Letter to Charles Hammond, 1821)

A chief ingredient in the structuring of government by the
leaders of America was recognition of man's sinful nature.
Government on the one hand has to be able to marshall great
powers when needed for national defense, but on the other
hand needs to be decentralized to the maximum extent practical to be a tool for individual liberty. Power of government is
not only divided and limited by the federal and state constitutions but decentralized. The great majority of powers are kept
locally and at the state level. The powers were split up as
checks against one another—executive, legislative and judicial
with the citizens having the power of change through the ballot box. The military was kept under control for the safety of
individual liberty. Most alarming at the end of the second
century is the manner in which bureaucratic planners and
their agents are functioning—a manner akin to militarist!

XI. Taxes limited for liberty's sake.

"He has erected a multitude of New Offices, and sent
hither swarms of officers to harass our people, and eat
out their substance."

(Declaration of Independence)

This traditional American philosophy goes hand in hand

with the right of the common people to retain the fruits of their labor for self-support and to own property. Tyranny through taxation is most oppressive and dangerous because it changes the balance of power and makes the citizens servants of government tyranny itself.

"Indeed, we cannot too often inculcate upon you our desires, that all extraordinary grants and expensive measures may, upon all occasions, as much as possible, be avoided. The public money of this country is the toil and labor of the people . . . reasonable frugality ought to be observed. And we would recommend particularly, the strictest care and the utmost firmness to prevent all unconstitutional draughts upon the public treasury."

> Instructions of Town of Braintree, Mass.
> (To their legislative Representatives, 1765)

"As a very important source of strength and security, cherish public credit . . . use it as sparingly as possible . . . ; avoiding likewise the accumulation of debt . . . in time of Peace . . . discharge the Debts which unavoidable wars may have occasioned, not ungenerously throwing upon posterity the burden which we ourselves ought to bear."

> President George Washington
> (Farewell Address)

XII. The majority limited for the sake of individual liberty.

The Constitution was designed to remedy existing injustices perpetrated " . . . by the superior force of an interested and overbearing majority."

> *The Federalist* (No. 10, by Madison)

" . . . this sacred principle . . ." (Majority must respect Minority's rights) "All, too, will bear in mind this sacred principle, that though the will of the majority is in all cases to prevail, that will to be rightful must be reasonable; that the minority possess their equal rights, which equal law must protect, and to violate would be oppression."

> (President Jefferson's First Inaugural Address)

"I believe . . . that the majority, oppressing an individual, is guilty of a crime, abuses its strength, and by acting on the law of the strongest breaks up the foundations of society . . ."

Thomas Jefferson
(Letter to Dupont de Nemours, 1816)

REAL AND CERTAIN PRINCIPLES TO FIGHT FOR

Our founding fathers rejected democracy and chose instead to form a republic—a constitutionally limited government of the representative type. The limits established by our Constitution were specifically to protect the individual's unalienable rights, to protect minorities against violations by the government, by monopolies or by others.

"Each of us has a natural right—from God—to defend his person, his liberty and his property. These are the three basic requirements of life, the preservation of any one of them is completely dependent upon the preservation of the other two."

THE LAW, by Frederic Bastiat, Paris, June 1850

Understanding the conflict and the specific principles of liberty we will again have a commitment and a faith so vibrant and so compelling that our contribution will more than match the fanaticism and corruption and total power of those who would destroy human freedoms.

We must never, never give up. Nobility never gives up a noble cause and throws in the towel, so to speak. It can be fun, it is work, it is worthy, it is God's will, and it is much better than anarchy or chains. It is the only hope for our little children and grandchildren as they look to us and sincerely believe that we are trustworthy. For those of us who have failed to be active, it is to our shame, but we can correct this. The Pledge of Allegiance still says, "One Nation Under God." By fulfilling our civic as well as Christian duties we can lend new credence to this noble pledge, the same duty seen by the leaders in 1776.

The frustration and confusion over decay and loss of power in America today will be corrected when we see the inconsistency of taking the God of liberty and judgment and moral absolutes out of formal training; and nothing short of a return of these truths as they were taught for most of our nation's history will save us! With this truth inculcated again into the political body of our nation, nothing can destroy us.

Henceforth this urgent call to re-educate ourselves, the young and old alike, for liberty! Portions of a series of essays first published in *Boston Gazette*, 1765 by John Adams:

> Let us . . . cherish, therefore, the means of knowledge. Let us dare to read, think, speak, and write. Let every order and decree among the people rouse their attention and animate their resolution. Let them all become attentive to the grounds and principles of government. ..

Strengthen the heart and mind and soul anew with the harsh realities of collectivism. John Adams further states:

> Let us read and recollect and impress upon our souls the views and ends of our own immediate forefathers, in exchanging their native country for a dreary, inhospitable wilderness. Let us examine the nature of that power and the cruelty of that oppression, which drove them from their homes. Recollect their amazing fortitude, their bitter sufferings,—the hunger, the nakedness, the cold, which they patiently endured—the severe labors of clearing their grounds, building their houses, raising their provisions, amidst dangers. . ., before they had time or money or materials for commerce. Recollect the civil and religious principles and hopes and expectations which constantly supported and carried them through all hardships with patience and resignation.
>
> In such researches as these, let us all in our several departments cheerfully engage,—but especially the proper patrons and supporters of law, learning, and religion!

Clearly preach the fundamentals of the supernatural God Who knows our weaknesses and elevates His people one by one as they come to Him.

Let the pulpit resound with the doctrines and sentiments of religious liberty. Let us hear the danger of thraldom to our consciences from ignorance, extreme poverty, and dependence, in short, from civil and political slavery. Let us see delineated before us the true map of man. Let us hear the dignity of his nature, and the noble rank he holds among the works of God,—that consenting to slavery is a sacrilegious breach of trust, as offensive in the sight of God as it is derogatory from our own honor or interest or happiness,—and that God Almighty has promulgated from heaven, liberty, peace, and good-will to man!

Support the Constitution in its true and original meaning!!

Let the bar proclaim, "the laws, the rights, the generous plan of power" delivered down from remote antiquity,—inform the world of the mighty struggles and numberless sacrifices made by our ancestors in defence of freedom . . .

Abandon the irresponsible liberties which corrupt the minds and remove responsible curbs on personal behavior. Teach affirmatively the unique principles of American government, with individuals the bulwark responsible for their own destiny before God.

Let the colleges join their harmony in the same delightful concert. Let every declamation turn upon the beauty of liberty and virtue, and the deformity, turpitude, and malignity of slavery and vice (governmental evils from the standpoint of Free Man). Let the public disputations become researches into the grounds and nature and ends of government, and the means of preserving the good and demolishing the evil. Let the dialogues, and all the exercised, become the instruments of impressing on the tender mind, and of spreading and distributing far and wide, the ideas of right and the sensations of freedom.

Prepare and stand firm against wretched lies that would trick us into acquiescing where education is devoid of freedom's principles.

The following from Samuel Adams (1771 Essays *Boston Gazette*):

If the liberties of America are ever completely ruined, of which in my opinion there is the utmost danger, it will in all probability be the consequence of a mistaken notion of prudence, which leads men to acquiesce in measures of the most destructive tendency for the sake of present ease. When designs are form'd to rase the very foundation of a free government, those few who are to erect their grandeur and fortunes upon the general ruin, will employ every art to sooth the devoted people into a state of indolence, inattention and security, which is forever the fore-runner of slavery—They are alarmed at nothing so much, as attempts to awaken the people to jealousy and watchfulness; and it has been an old game played over and over again, to hold up the men who would rouse their fellow citizens and countrymen to a sense of their real danger, and spirit them to the most zealous activity in the use of all proper means for the preservation of the public liberty, as "pretended patriots," "intemperate politicians," rash, hot-headed men, Incendiaries, wretched desperadoes, who, as was said of the best of men, would turn the world upside down, or have done it already.

Teach and work for society under God with responsible liberty and justice for all. Samuel Adams continues:

The liberties of our Country, the freedom of our civil constitution are worth defending at all hazards: And it is our duty to defend them against all attacks. We haye receiv'd them as a fair Inheritance from our worthy Ancestors: They purchas'd them for us with toil and danger and expence of treasure and blood; and have transmitted them to us with care and diligence. It will bring an everlasting mark of infamy on the present generation, enlightened as it is, if we should suffer them to be wrested from us . . . without a struggle; or be cheated out of them by the artifices of false and designing men. Of the latter we are in most danger . . . Let us therefore be aware of it. Let us contemplate our forefathers and posterity; and resolve to maintain the rights bequeath'd to us from the former, for the sake of the latter.—Instead of sitting down satisfied with the efforts we have already made, which is the wish of our enemies, the necessity of the times, more than ever, calls for our utmost circumspection, deliberation, fortitude and perseverance. Let us remember, that "if we suffer tamely a lawless attack upon our liberty, we encourage it, and involve others in our doom." It is a very serious consideration, which should deeply impress our minds, that millions yet unborn may be the miserable sharers in the event.

In the tradition of liberty and independence, be self-taught. Take upon yourself the responsibility of your family's liberty.

128

CONGREGATIONAL HARMONY

A Manual
for
Deacons and Church Officers

By David A. Norris

CONTENTS

4th Printing—July, 1977

Recommended only for churches which are locally
governed with the aid of representative leaders controlled by the congregation.

PREFACE

It was my joy and privilege to be David Norris' pastor for five years. Several of these happy and fruitful years Brother Norris served on the Board of Deacons with dedication and distinction. His counsel is Biblical, practical, and workable. I heartily recommend this booklet. There is so little sound literature available of a practical nature on the subject for laymen to use, it ought to have wide circulation.

A word should be included about the Norris family. His precious and dedicated wife adds to Dave's effectiveness as a counselor. And their three lovely daughters exemplify and bear witness to a Christ-honoring home.

L. Duane Brown, Ph.D., State Representative
Pennsylvania Association of Regular Baptist Churches
Lewisburg, Pennsylvania

This book was brought to my attention just prior to my being contacted by the Pulpit Committee of Campus Baptist Church. One logical question: "Do they operate in the manner as set forth in this book?"

Now, after having gone through the process of interview, candidating, and responding to the Lord's definite leading to become pastor of Campus Baptist Church, I am proud and happy to report that the Board of Deacons and the Congregation follow the principles and practices set forth herein. And that makes for a happy and unifying fellowship and blessings from the Lord!

It is with great personal pride and pleasure, therefore, that I recommend this book. Because of its Biblical basis, those who read it and follow it will find it most helpful.

Dr. Ben Strohbehn, Pastor
Campus Baptist Church
Ames, Iowa

ACKNOWLEDGEMENTS

It has been my privilege to be associated with many successful people who have done their best for God in the local church. This includes both pastors and laymen from many walks of life. I believe, in one way or another, each has made a contribution to the ideas here.

Henry Drummond's book "The Greatest Thing in the World," "The Hyles Church Manual" by Dr. Jack Hyles, and Dr. Paul R. Jackson's book "The Doctrine and Administration of the Church," all excellent resources, were very helpful.

I am grateful to Dr. L. Duane Brown, former pastor of our local church, and Rev. Donald Brong, representative for the General Association of Regular Baptist Churches of Iowa, who have been most helpful in reviewing the material and giving of their experience to improve the manual.

David A. Norris

INTRODUCTION

The purpose of this booklet is to focus on ways that Bible-believing congregations can work in harmony and avoid much of the destructive strife that plagues churches.

Knowledge of the strife in churches seems so universal and accepted that it almost would lead us to believe that it is a necessary part of church life, but this is not true. Both the Bible conservatives and the liberals have church problems, but their solutions may be different, depending on the structure of their church government. Many of the Bible conservative congregations are organized into independent churches. They survived the trend toward liberalism in large part by virtue of the fact that they were independent and not subject to outside management. It is very important that locally-governed churches make a special effort to avoid needless strife and be prepared to handle it locally when it comes with a minimum of damage. The other churches can frequently handle their problems best by passing them on to some non-local authority to which they are in submission.

For Christians to live in harmony is very important. The Bible is explicit about the purpose of and the advantages in doing things via the local church. The local Bible church is the channel for our efforts, in order to receive a maximum multiplying affect in the service of our Lord and Saviour and Creator, in evangelism, in spiritual maturing of Christians, and in missionary outreach. This rightly receives the attention of much of our Christian literature.

This booklet has been compiled largely from experiences of an independent fundamental Baptist deacon board. Some of the lessons learned were learned the hard way. The purpose of this booklet is to share with others ways to promote harmony and to avoid divisive contentions that can swell up

from minor issues and impair the important God-given ministry of the church. There are, of course, many problems
that leaders within the church will encounter for which the
only guideline is a cautious searching of the Scriptures,
prayer, and waiting upon wisdom and direction from the
Lord. With reference to the subject generally, there seems to
be very little reading material for deacons or a similarly des-
ignated group of leaders within the church, who are the human keys to a harmonious, spiritually prosperous, and
growing church. For this reason the deacon board functions
elaborated on in this booklet are directed to a rather nar-
rowness of purpose: promoting harmony in the church.

This manual is addressed mainly to Christians—those who
have already acknowledged that they are sinners (Eccls.
7:20; Rom. 3:10, 23), have recognized that they cannot save
themselves (Rom. 6:23; Eph. 2:8, 9); and, in true repent-
ance, have asked Christ to be their Saviour from sin (John
1:12; 3:16; 5:24).

If you have not received Christ as your Saviour, you are
not "at peace" with God. You are (Rom. 5:6, 10) in need of
being reconciled to Him (II Cor. 5:20b). You need to ac-
knowledge your sin and trust Christ as your Saviour. You
need to come to Jesus Christ, the only true Source of lasting
peace (Eph. 2:14).

But the Bible indicates that Christians, even though they
have believed in and received Christ for salvation, still sin (I
John 1:8-10). Many Christians hold hatred, fear, resentment,
jealousy, and malice toward others. As a result, fellowship
with these persons and the Lord is broken, joy is lost, and
God's peace is not enjoyed. Confession of sin (I John 1:9)
and forsaking of one's sinful ways in obedience to the Lord
and His Word (Prov. 28:13) are necessary if the Christian is
to enjoy God's peace (Gal. 5:22, Rom. 15:33).

CHAPTER I – BACKGROUND FOR CHURCH POLICY

The codification of Scriptures on this subject is beyond the intent of this booklet. We touch only briefly upon three basic Bible teachings: carnal man, church leaders, and common sense according to Scriptures.

Carnal Man

The carnal or selfish nature of man with his volatile tendencies is an element in every church. World history is a reflection of man generally, and history is dominated by strife, wars, and continual problems in civic affairs and business, as well as in church life. The Bible points out that the best of people, when out of fellowship with God, can get off on a tangent, and what do we have? We have murmuring, feuding, splitting of friendships, and loss of trust.

I Corinthians 3:1-3: "And I, brethren, could not speak unto you as unto spiritual, but as unto carnal, even as unto babes in Christ. I have fed you with milk, and not with meat: for hitherto ye were not able to bear it; neither yet now are ye able. For ye are yet carnal: for whereas there is among you envying, and strife, and divisions, are ye not carnal, and walk as men?"

Romans 7:14-17: "For we know that the law is spiritual: but I am carnal, sold under sin. For that which I do I allow not: for what I would, that do I not; but what I hate, that do I. If then I do that which I would not, I consent unto the law that it is good. Now then it is no more I that do it, but sin that dwelleth in me."

Acts 6:1: "And in those days, when the number of the dis-

9

ciples was multiplied, there arose a murmuring of the Grecians against the Hebrews, because their widows were neglected in the daily ministration."

Church Leaders

Deacons compose a board of select members (from a congregation) who are hopefully spiritually mature, not volatile, to help in the administration of church affairs, including the minimizing and the preventing of problems.

Acts 6:3: "Wherefore, brethren, look we out among you seven men of honest report, full of the Holy Spirit and wisdom, whom ye may appoint over this business."

It is important that all deacon nominees are selected from those in the congregation who are spiritually aright with God.

I Corinthians 2:15: "But he that is spiritual judgeth all things, yet he himself is judged of no man."

Galatians 5:22-26: "But the fruit of the Spirit is love, joy, peace, long-suffering, gentleness, goodness, faith, meekness, temperance: against such there is no law. And they that are Christ's have crucified the flesh with the affections and lusts. If we live in the Spirit, let us also walk in the Spirit. Let us not be desirous of vain glory, provoking one another, envying one another."

Common Sense According to Scriptures.

In view of men's tendencies, the use of common sense and good planning cannot be overemphasized. The Scriptures refer to this in many ways that pertain.

I Corinthians 2:15: "But he that is spiritual judgeth all things, . . ."

I Corinthians 14:40: "Let all things be done decently and in order."

Titus 1:5: "For this cause left I thee in Crete, that thou

• shouldest set in order the things that are wanting, and ordain elders in every city, as I had appointed thee."

CHAPTER II
A MOST POWERFUL FORCE IN HUMAN AFFAIRS

The power of love:

I Corinthians 13:1-8a: "Though I speak with the tongues of men and of angels, and have not love, I am become as sounding brass, or a tinkling cymbal.
And though I have the gift of prophecy, and understand all mysteries, and all knowledge; and though I have all faith, so that I could remove mountains, and have not love, I am nothing.
And though I bestow all my goods to feed the poor, and though I give my body to be burned, and have not love, it profiteth me nothing.
Love suffereth long, and is kind; love envieth not; love vaunteth not itself, is not puffed up.
Doth not behave itself unseemly, seeketh not her own, is not easily provoked, thinketh no evil;
Rejoiceth not in iniquity, but rejoiceth in the truth;
Beareth all things, believeth all things, hopeth all things, endureth all things.
Love never faileth.

The question is not whether the pastor, the deacons, or other church members will make mistakes. All make mistakes; D. L. Moody and C. H. Spurgeon made mistakes. The question is this: will we display the fruits of a spiritual person and work to smooth it out and improve things in the future, or will we be a carnal person and magnify it and make it worse? The statement has been made that the job of a newspaper editor is to take a mole hill and make a mountain out of it. This statement is unfair when applied to all news copy writers, but it is, unfortunately, true of some Christians and newspaper personnel as well.

The power of God's love, when applied to the lives of church members, is the greatest single remedy for church problems. We need to be constantly reminded and to remind one another to be kindhearted and to be conscious of the need of this power in all church matters. If we yield to carnality, we lose the wonderful fruits of the Spirit and the power of love that make for a thriving church and happy Christians.

God's Word is quite specific and broad when instructing on the subject of charity or love.

Patience.........Love suffereth long
Kindness.........And is kind
Generosity......Love envieth not
Humility........Love vaunteth not itself, is not puffed up
Courtesy........Doth not behave itself unseemly
Unselfishness.....Seeketh not her own
Good Temper....Is not easily provoked
Guilelessness.....Thinketh no evil
Sincerity........Rejoiceth not in iniquity, but rejoiceth
                 in the truth

A prime responsibility of deacons and other church leaders is to be bearers of love and to be alert to individual instances where in a humble way they should emphasize the practice of charity among others. I Peter 4:8 says love covers a multitude of sins. The talebearer has no place in God's favor. Since all, literally all, Christians make mistakes, it is God's power, and His alone, that will bring success and progress to the church ministry. If we know of something that would hinder or hurt the reputation of one of God's children, it should be buried and never, except in the process of board review for discipline or personal counseling, be reported to anyone else!!!

Chapter 13 of 1st Corinthians comes down hard on anyone who soft peddles the command and the need of church members working in the power of God's love, in stating " . . . though I give my body to be burned and have not love, it profiteth me nothing." Certainly Christian martyrdom is one of the greatest of all sacrifices, we would all agree, and yet God's Word says if we should perform such a service and have not love, we are nothing.

Guilelessness and sincerity cannot be dismissed lightly.

Guilelessness is the grace for suspicious people. To possess it is a great secret of personal influence. Progress comes when we believe in people in spite of their weakness and encourage them for the better rather than allow things to degenerate in an atmosphere of suspicion.

"Rejoiceth not in iniquity, but rejoiceth in the truth." This is a hard truth and to fail to see and live it, destroys fellowship with God and service to man. It includes more strictly the self-restraint which refuses to make capital out of others' faults. Real charity or love delights not in exposing the weakness of others, but "covereth all things." Even the disciplinary action thrust upon the deacon board must be motivated and administered in love.

CHAPTER III
DEACON SELECTION AND REQUIREMENTS

The importance of selecting deacons from the more mature and sensible men in the church is obvious, but the method of selection may not be so obvious.

A. Because of the fact that the people who are doing the bulk of the church work are most likely to know who is qualified and who is not qualified, it is advisable that a select nominating committee composed of active church workers finalize the slate of candidates for the congregation. Some churches have a nominating committee composed of two deacons, two trustees, and two members from the congregation as a whole, selected by their respective group for this purpose. The congregation should be strongly encouraged, if not required, to make their nominations in advance to the nominating committee because last minute nominations from the floor run the risk of getting a candidate who is unqualified or unwilling to serve.

B. Before new church members are considered as deacons, they should be proven by exposure to the congregation in lesser capacities for at least a year. As in every phase of our society, a few enter our churches with very impressive credentials, but are not qualified for leadership; and there are a few who literally prey on the unsuspecting—who are living in sin and, who in positions of church leadership, do great harm.

C. The qualifications for deacons are laid out in Acts 6 and I Timothy 3; their qualifications should be based upon spirituality, loyalty, and desire to work. Selection based upon community prestige, financial success, etc., of candidates is a mistake.

CHAPTER IV – DEACON RESPONSIBILITIES

A. Duties. Following is a partial list of deacons' duties, some of which may or may not fit a particular church situation.
  1. Visit shut-ins of the church.
  2. Serve as an advisory board. However, final authority is vested in church members—deacons only advise. This is a humble position.
  3. Serve as pastor's helpers.
  4. Serve as personal workers: at the invitation following the pastor's message, at visitation, and in everyday witnessing, with the ability and desire to lead others to Christ.
  5. Counsel, at the request of the pastor and board, with carnal Christians, trouble-makers, fault-finders, and those who have an unforgiving spirit.
  6. Oversee the entire church program—on all committees, etc.
  7. Serve as pulpit committee when seeking a pastor.
B. Deacons' meetings
  1. Meetings should be scheduled regularly and should always include prayer.
  2. The meeting agenda should always be prepared in advance.
  3. Larger church boards can benefit by having subcommittees work in specific areas and report back with recommendations to the entire board.
  4. After decisions are reached by the board, these must be supported by all members of the board. This is an elementary principle that should never be violated. Questions under consideration should be thoroughly discussed, including all advantages and disadvantages

that seem significant to each and every deacon. In this way, hopefully, not only will the decision be the best one, but when every deacon contributes his ideas, the board will have an overview of the different ideas and concerns that could be expected from the congregation as a whole.

After all the opinions have been aired and a decision made on a recommendation to make to the congregation, *every single deacon*, no matter what his opinion was during the decision-making process, must support the decision both privately and publicly. Violating this flaunts all the principles of order and common sense and destroys the deacon board as an instrument for leadership and harmony in the church.

5. Deacons' business does not go beyond the meeting to wives or to anyone else.

C. Local church and deacons

1. Teamwork is essential. Great churches have no stars. Preaching and teaching and other duties are divided, lay leadership is accented, and Christ is given the Headship.

2. The pastor's position in the church.
   a. The pastor serves as "shepherd" or church leader. Ezekiel 34, I Peter 5, I Timothy 3.
   b. The pastor is in God's vineyard to cultivate it. He is responsible to God for the spiritual welfare of His people.
   c. Pastors do not always have personalities pleasing to us, nor do they always do their work in ways which we prefer. However, we are admonished to ". . . esteem them very highly in love for their work's sake." (1 Thess. 5:13)

3. The pastor is a person.
   a. Sheep need tending, but so do shepherds.
      Acts 14:15: "We also are men of like passions with you, and preach unto you that ye should turn from these vanities unto the living God, which made heaven, and earth, and the sea, and all things that are therein."
   b. God does not expect pastors to behave better than other Christians. All Christians, preachers and lay-

men ought to behave in a manner that draws respect, but we all fail sometimes. The miracle is that God enables us to love, forgive, and support one another.

c. The pastor is at a disadvantage, being somewhat isolated from laymen's experiences and everyday attitudes, and therefore thinks differently than laymen.

D. Deacons—the pastor's helpers

1. Artificial status to pastors is harmful, so avoid this.
   a. A good pastor is a man with good motives and who tries, but he is *not* perfect.
   b. To magnify the pastor by giving him an artificial status is bad. It exposes him to the temptation of pride, can isolate him from the team-level fellowship needed in a great church, and can cause the people to judge him by a harsher standard than they place on themselves.
   c. The pastor needs love, prayer, understanding, and fellowship, without being expected to give up his independence as a pastor.

2. Deacons—the pastor's antennae
   a. Deacons should be eyes and ears for the pastor and the board and be sensitive to any indications of developing problems or needs within the church.
   b. Deacons should not keep any information or criticisms of significance from the pastor, but should advise him in a considerate and loving manner.
   c. Wise pastors seek deacons' advice on hard decisions, and wise deacons give advice without expecting the pastor to do as they advise.

3. Deacons—the pastor's shield
   a. A church family, like a family, are loyal to one another, and deacons owe a particular loyalty to the pastor. Errors are counseled on a person-to-person basis. Deacons never criticize the pastor, other deacons, or church workers publicly!!! Criticism of the pastor by others should be muted to the best of the deacons' ability, e.g., remind them that the pastor is human, sincere, etc.
   b. Deacons should understand the vulnerability of any

human being in the pastor's job. Deacons should understand the terrible, destructive power of people who are constantly criticizing and fault-finding. These people usually add to the tragedy and end up destroying their own homes by not giving their children a firm base on which to grow.

c. If some individual or committee, e.g., music committee, should grow in power and authority and reduce, for example, the music director to a slave and the pastor to a figurehead, the deacons, after prayerful counsel, not the pastor, should perform the surgery or see that adequate adjustments are made. Such surgery usually involves carnal Christians who will be bitter. Deacons are easier to replace, come the next church election, and it is better to have the individual or committee upset with the deacons rather than with the pastor.

E. Deacons and music. Music, perhaps more than anything else, can have a stimulating and helpful, or depressing and harmful effect on the pastor and/or the congregation.

1. Pastor and deacons should see that the pastor is the pastor of the music as well as the other programs of the church.

a. The purpose of the music is to prepare the pastor and the congregation for the preaching of the Word of God. All those participating in the music program should understand this most important aspect of the church service.

b. The music director should be able to carry out the music program on his own, but he must have the capacity and disposition to serve with the approval of and make changes upon the suggestion of the pastor.

c. The music committee should include a deacon and other members who, though not necessarily professional musicians, have a deep concern for the church policy on music as well as a good music program.

d. Pastoral guidance could include going through the song book and approving songs, for the director's benefit, which are acceptable for congregational singing.

CHAPTER V – PASTOR'S VACATION

A. Paid vacation is very important. The length varies, but how hard the pastor works should be an influencing factor. It should compare favorably with other professions.

Example: Federal employees' vacation schedule
(five-day work week):

1 to 3 years employment	13 days yearly
3 to 15 years employment	20 days yearly
over 15 years employment	26 days yearly
8 paid holidays	

13 days sick leave per year—accumulative; those not used carry over to next year

B. It is good if the vacation includes some genuine rest and time spent with the entire family. The pastor and family should not come back to the church activities exhausted.

CHAPTER VI
OUTREACH BEYOND THE LOCAL CHURCH

A. Pastor and the traveling choir, etc.
  1. Exchange of talent and ideas between churches and church organizations is helpful and stimulating.
  2. The pastor should keep the deacons informed on the details of outside opportunities which he feels deserve his and the church's support.
  3. Pastors should not accept double compensation from two employers without their both knowing about it.
  4. A pastor can gain much support and understanding by providing replacements when taking out-

side assignments on local church time and considering their financial needs the same as he considers his own.

CHAPTER VII – THOUGHTS FOR THE PASTOR

It is important as pastor to understand that in the final analysis *the tertiary force for progress lies in the membership as a whole,* and he should, therefore, seek God's help and try constantly to avoid needless actions that could destroy people's confidence in his leadership. When confidence wanes some of the congregation begin to see their pastor as a less spiritual man than when he first arrived. In reality he is just as spiritual and just as good a preacher, but some of the congregation begin to tune this out.

It may be well on occasion to remind the congregation as a pastor that you are not perfect and you are doing your best but need their understanding, prayers, and help. As parents we have cultivated this attitude with our children. This is done by reminding them we are not perfect, that we are doing our best as parents, but in a very real sense they are in God's hands. In this way, without relenting in any way in our duty as earthly parents, they respect us for our honesty and see in finality they are responsible to God, the perfect Father.

The isolation and other natural tendencies sometimes felt by the pastor give the temptation felt by all to tell things which, if heard by critical ears, would be passed on to others and cause great loss of support within the congregation. Pastors should be especially cautious about criticizing other pastors of like faith. Since no one is perfect such criticism rendered carelessly tends to boomerang and reduce confidence all around.

The support of a loving, forgiving, understanding deacon board is very beneficial, but does not compare with the support of a congregation that sees their pastor as a man with a pure heart, sincerely working as their undershepherd.

CHAPTER VIII
BUSINESS MEETINGS AND DEACONS

A. Review ground rules with the congregation at least yearly. Preventive medicine is much better than the cure.

  1. Insist on kindness at all times to persons and issues involved in business meetings.

    a. God commands it and makes it possible.

    b. The power of the church is in love and forbearance.

    c. Rudeness and harsh words exhibit an unchristian spirit and destroy the atmosphere conducive to enjoyable worship and fellowship.

  2. It should be known that deacons are readily accessible personally to any who have suggestions or criticisms.

  3. All should realize they have a right to speak in opposition to the proposal under consideration during the discussion on the proposal.

  4. The principal of divine order should be followed and the husband, not the wife, should be the spokesman, on any issue that could possibly be controversial.

    I Corinthians 14:34, 35: "Let your women keep silence in the churches: for it is not permitted unto them to speak; but they are commanded to be under obedience, as also saith the law. And if they will learn any thing, let them ask their husbands at home: for it is a shame for women to speak in the church."

    I Timothy 2:12: "But I suffer not a woman to teach, not to usurp authority over the man, but to be in silence."

B. Prepare thoroughly for business meetings.
 1. The pastor should be present at deacons' and business meetings.
 2. The board should thoughtfully analyze all possible alternatives.
    a. Many church troubles are caused by a lack of thoughtfulness and proper planning on the part of the pastor and deacons. Sources and types of objections to recommendations, as well as benefits, should be considered.
    b. Use outside expert advice when needed.
 3. Notice should be given to the membership on big decisions prior to the business meeting.
    a. Always inform people with recommendations some two or three weeks prior to the business meeting. An informed membership is a trusting membership.
    b. Hold a hearing in advance of the business meeting for the church membership to comment on crucial recommendations, e.g., missionary budget, building plan, etc.
 4. A board spokesman should anticipate the types of questions that will be asked at the meeting and prepare his answers in advance.
C. The business meeting.
 1. All who want to speak should be given the opportunity.
 2. A spokesman should never display his temper.
    a. The spokesman who retaliates is often seen and penalized in the mind of meeting participants rather than the tormentors or thoughtless critics.
    b. A kind and gracious spirit glorifies God and the local church ministry.
 3. Opposition should never be encouraged. The goal is to hear out those who want to be heard and move to a decision supported by a strong majority.
 4. Some decisions receiving only marginal support should be reconsidered. A spokesman could ask the church to table important decisions involving

purchases, etc., when the church is almost equally divided, "Since the vote has been so close, I would like to entertain a motion that we rescind the action just taken, place the matter in the hands of the board of deacons, trustees, etc., for further study, in order that they might bring back a more suitable recommendation at our next business meeting." The purchase of a house or song books is not as important as unity in the church. (Eph. 4:3.)

CHAPTER IX – PULPIT COMMITTEE AND ITS WORK

Congregations that select and call their own pastor are able to secure special blessings of God through self-government, but this calls for considerable care and responsibility of every adult individual in the church membership. The decision is most important because of the long-term impact in the ministry of both the pastor and the church.

The goal of the Pulpit Committee should be to find God's man for the church. This requires working with the congregation in a way that is agreeable to the congregation in the procedures used and the candidate called. God ". . . gave some (churches) apostles; and some, prophets; and some, evangelists; and some, pastors and teachers; for the perfecting of the saints, for the work of the ministry" (Eph. 4:11-12a).

A. Prayer. I Thessalonians 5:17; James 1:5-6; Acts 6:1-4; Acts 13:1-3.

1. The deacons or Pulpit Committee should constantly bathe their proceedings in prayer.
2. The congregation should be called upon to give special emphasis in their prayers that God's will for a pastor might be known. This could include a special Day of Prayer at the outset and continual reminders to the congregation through the bulletin and from the pulpit.

B. The congregation and Pulpit Committee.

1. Congregational Resolve.

   As the Pulpit Committee considers the best procedure to use in getting a new pastor, it is important that some consideration be given the question, "Is the congregation ready spiritually and mentally to call a pastor?" Sometimes events preceding the need of a new pastor will leave some members in the congregation looking at each other instead of being resolved to work in a positive manner as a part of the church team. Until the congregation is settled down before God, there is a real danger that the efforts to get a new pastor will abort or, if successful, the ministry of the new pastor may be adversely affected due to the lack of support.

2. Those who care, share.

An all-important factor throughout the pastor-calling-process is communications. Pulpit Committees who understand this and who care, share. There is no end to the apprehensions that may exist within the congregation. Are the deacons going to work this way or that in getting a new pastor? Are the deacons going to recommend a candidate too quickly? Are they going to delay too long? Church members who want to put God's will first and see their responsibility to work and support the pastor with a good attitude should share ideas, which they think are significant, with the Pulpit Committee. Two-way communications can clear up or minimize apprehensions and the Pulpit Committee should be sure that the congregation is informed and their ideas sought in advance. Decisions on the procedures and timing can be improved through an assessment and consideration of the mood of the congregation. Support of the congregation can be maximized by:

a. Inviting the church members to come to a specially set meeting for the purpose of getting ideas on possible candidates, things that concern them, ideas on procedures to use, etc.

b. Tentatively agreeing as a Board on the method of getting and calling a pastor, then presenting the plan to the church and encouraging any member to attend the next deacons' meeting to make suggestions.

    c. Informing the congregation throughout the various stages of the process. Do not proceed to the next stage unless and until you have the support of the congregation. Allow the time needed for God's Word to work in hearts and the Spirit, with God's love, to restore fellowship where strained.

    d. Avoid giving the impression as a Pulpit Committee that you are trying to sell a candidate by adding speculative laurels to him. Use the considered testimony of others who have good judgment and who know, if deemed wise.

C. Prospecting

  1. Define what you are looking for in a pastor.

    Evaluate as a Board the weaknesses and strengths within the church and just what type of pastoral emphasis and abilities would best complement future progress.

  2. Selecting potential candidates.

    "Where no counsel is, the people fall: but in the multitude of counsellors there is safety" (Prov. 11:14).

    a. Seek recommendations from sound church association leaders whose judgment is respected and who have many contacts and would not, because of their position or commitment, be a candidate. Contact these men without collaboration and ask them to consider the church and the need and to suggest two or three men they think would be the best possible candidates.

  3. Screening prospects.

    Secure a number of names of potential candidates and give consideration to those most frequently recommended. The opinion of leaders outside the church, added to what is known within the Pulpit Committee, should help to reduce the list to what seems to be the best five or six possibilities.

D. Procedure

  1. Agree on the procedure to use that seems best for the congregation in getting acquainted with and calling a candidate. Advise the congregation of the procedure and give them the reasons this appears to be the best alternative. Seek ideas from the congregation in ad-

vance that may improve the way it is done. Two of the most common procedures are:

a. To expose and recommend one man at a time to the congregation. I believe this to be the best method, particularly if prospecting and screening are well done and the congregation agrees that this is the best approach.

b. To present two or three candidates and see which one seems most popular with the congregation. I do not normally suggest this because it may be hard on the candidates who are rejected and hurt their present ministry. Often, the best man may not be willing to be considered through such a procedure. There is further disadvantage because popularity cannot be a safe measure unless the congregation gets considerable exposure to each candidate and this takes some months to accomplish.

2. Communicate directly with the prospective candidate. Invite the consideration of the best man until a possible candidate is secured and follow through with a two-way communication. You may invite the man to come to the church as a pulpit supply. If reaction is favorable, the Pulpit Committee can invite him back again to be considered by the congregation as a candidate.

E. Is he God's man? Do the candidate and the church fit together? The earlier screening process should have answered the basic questions—is he doctrinally sound; does he have a good family situation; is he a practical man with whom the congregation will prosper spiritually and become active in service? What are his study habits, ideas on counselling, etc.?

Sometime prior to the time the man comes as a candidate, it is advisable that some of the Pulpit Committee visit the man's present church and home to verify and get impressions of the work being accomplished there. It is good to seek his counsel on the best way to explain your presence in the church. Although a Pulpit Committee visit may enhance his ministry there, care should be taken so his ministry will not be hurt. Comments from others who have been in the home should be sought as well. It would be wise to obtain a credit report through the local credit bureau—one measure of his personal business habits.

When the prospect comes the first time to fill the pulpit or as a candidate, he probably will have many questions. He will want to get as complete a picture as possible of the church, its potential, its problems, the community, etc. The church members should know well in advance that the pulpit supply may be called back at a later date as a candidate. They should be encouraged to attend as he fills the pulpit. The Board or Pulpit Committee as a whole should have a thorough get-acquainted-session with the candidate and his wife. Eating together and other social activities offer good opportunities for this. If possible the visit might cover two or three days, including a potluck, social gathering with all the officers and teachers of the church, etc. The training union could be set aside for all the church to hear a brief message on the family and the home from the possible candidate, then open up the meeting for questions from any of the church members.

Care should be taken to be sure that the schedule leaves no impressions upon the congregation of trying to over-sell the man or favoring members with his presence. Some prospects will favor staying in a home, some prefer a motel provided by the church.

Some member of the Pulpit Committee may be delegated the task of showing the prospect and his wife the community. This is a good time to gather personal information, salary considerations, challenges and problems in the local church, and the candidate's present church.

Realizing that God has chosen to use the church with fallible men and women, is to contemplate one of the greatest proofs there is of God's power. The pastor-congregation relationship, like a happy family, needs to be a relationship of love: first, love of God and second, between the members. "And above all these things put on charity, which is the bond of perfectness" (Col. 3:14).

There is security and strength in the relationship because there is love and all the participants are good forgivers. Shortcomings are dealt with using understanding and communication and all concerned grow spiritually, mentally, and in effectiveness as a part of a team serving

God. It is not automatic—it takes work and a conscious understanding of the process whereby we bring glory to God through forgiving, growing and constantly striving to do better as a church team.

Every effort should be made to see that the man gets sufficient exposure before the church, in order that the Pulpit Committee will have ample evidence that he may be the right man before he is even considered officially as a candidate. Do the people like his personality; will the congregation work together and go forward under his preaching? Personal exposure by itself would be insufficient to make such an important decision. Testimony of others about the candidate's past ministry is very important. Is his level of development consistent with the challenge in your church?

F. Candidate comes

When the man comes as a candidate, most of the work by the Pulpit Committee has been done. The congregation should have at least a two or three-week notice of the day when the man will conduct the services as a candidate. The congregational vote on the candidate should follow as soon as practical. If the call is extended, normally the candidate will want to know what the vote was before he makes the final decision in his own mind as to God's will in the matter. The votes should be by ballot.

G. When a pastor leaves

When a pastor leaves a church, the departure should be dealt with tenderly and with love. This goes a long way in assuring God's blessing when calling a new pastor.

CONCLUSION

In quoting Dr. Paul R. Jackson, "The church is a group ruled by its own majority vote. Neither the pastor nor the deacons can rule the church. This is clear from Matthew 18:17 where the church is the final authority in discipline. It is also evident from Acts 15 where the 'whole church' determined the vital decision on true doctrine. The church has divinely provided officers and leaders, but the Lord has chosen to rest the final power in the entire group, subject to His own Headship.

"It is evident, therefore, that the Lord has designed the church with internal, interlocking powers and responsibilities. The church is to be subject to the pastor. Yet the pastor is subject to the church, in another sense, for he is called by them and may be disciplined by them.

"There is no problem here except for those who will not be subject to the Head of the church. It is not difficult for a Bible-taught church to be subject to the overseer or pastor that God has sent. Neither is it difficult for a faithful pastor to be sensitive to the will of God's people. What a lovely and delightful relationship exists between pastor, deacons, and people when all are subject to Christ the Head.

"It is vital that this happy relationship should always be evident in each church. When there is jealousy, bitterness, self-seeking and strife, and testimony of the Lord suffers, saints and sinners are caused to stumble, and the church loses its power to be a blessing because the Holy Spirit is grieved. Pastor and people must both recognize that the honor of the Lord and the welfare of His church must take precedence over personal differences. Let us suffer wrong. Let us 'lose face.' But the Lord must not be dishonored, His church be divided, or sinners be offended."

Any group involved in decision making will make mistakes. A congregation respects, however, the Board that faces up to its mistakes with corrections and treats its tormentors with sincere Christian love. This goes a long way toward minimizing the bad impressions new Christians or others might get when trouble comes.

The policies outlined in this booklet have been found to be very helpful. I pray sincerely that God may use some of these ideas to help you in your effort to be a more effective church leader for His glory.

David A. Norris

WHAT READERS SAY ABOUT
CONGREGATIONAL HARMONY!

Tremendously helpful! Other books emphasize programs; this one puts the finger on the heart of the matter—the people. It has helped our deacons to realize their main responsibility and to act accordingly to preserve congregational harmony. God is using the insight gained from this booklet in the lives of our church leadership. Praise Him!

Donald Kusmaul, Pastor
Calvary Baptist Church
Emporia, Kansas

"Congregational Harmony" booklets have been very helpful for my Board members. It's concise and covers what's needed on the subject.

Leland W. Anderson, Pastor
West Des Moines Open Bible Church
West Des Moines, Iowa

Every person who is a church officer should read this manual. A great deal of misunderstanding could be avoided if those who have oversight in our churches were familiar with it. I wish I had gotten this manual much sooner.

Dr. Bruce A. Beasley
Children's Dentistry
Mount Vernon, Washington

I believe it is one of the most effective lay ministry booklets ever printed. Every deacon and trustee should prayerfully read!

P. A. Stewart, Director
Christ for Everyone Inc.
New Era, Michigan

"Congregational Harmony" is assigned reading for all members of our Board of Deacons. It offers positive Biblical instruction on the roles and responsibilities of those entrusted with leadership in a local church.

H. C. Smith, Jr., Pastor
Emmanuel Evangelical Free Church
Burbank, California

The book "Congregational Harmony," a manual for deacons and Church officers, is unique. The book fills an obvious gap because we are given insight of Church function from a member, rather than by a Pastor. Pastors and professors of Theology often miss the view of the laborer who is also involved in the mundane, the everyday problems of life. The book presents a view of the Church from a beautiful perspective, that is, from the membership looking toward the pastor. Our Church has made it a matter of policy that anyone holding any office in the Church must read this valuable work. We thank God for the scholarly approach, the valuable content, and for the wonderful purpose of harmony for which this book is intended.

Keith W. Rose, Pastor
Hickory Street Baptist Church
Scranton, Pennsylvania

TWO IN ONE BOOK!